Books written by Jack Hartman

Trust God for Your Finances 1983 (over 175,000 copies in print)
Nuggets of Faith 1984
One Hundred Years from Today 1985
How to Study the Bible 1985
Never, Never Give Up 1994
Quiet Confidence in the Lord 1996

Books co-authored with Judy Hartman

Increased Energy and Vitality 1994
God's Wisdom Is Available to You 2001
Exchange Your Worries for God's Perfect Peace 2003
Unshakable Faith in Almighty God 2004
Receive Healing from the Lord 2006
What Does God Say? 2008
Victory Over Adversity 2009
God's Joy Regardless of Circumstances 2009
A Close and Intimate Relationship with God 2010
Overcoming Fear 2011
Effective Prayer 2011
God's Instructions for Growing Older 2012
You Can Hear the Voice of God 2012
God's Plan for Your Life 2013
Reverent Awe of God 2013
Glorious Eternal Life in Heaven 2014
Live Continually in the Presence of God 2014
The Rapture and the Second Coming of Christ 2015
God Lives in the Heart of Every Christian 2015

Scripture Meditation Cards
with accompanying CDs (1996-2000)
co-authored by Jack and Judy Hartman

A Closer Relationship with the Lord
Continually Increasing Faith in God
Enjoy God's Wonderful Peace
Financial Instructions from God
Find God's Will for Your Life
Freedom from Worry and Fear
God Is Always with You
Our Father's Wonderful Love
Receive God's Blessings in Adversity
Receive Healing from the Lord

God Lives in the Heart of Every Christian

Jack and Judy Hartman

Lamplight Ministries, Inc., Dunedin, Florida

We are excited that you have chosen to read this book. Our prayer is that you will be gripped by God Himself through the Scripture that is contained in this book. We pray that God will speak to your heart and that you will meditate often on these great scriptural truths pertaining to *God living in your heart*. Our goal is to help you center every aspect of your life around the indwelling presence of God.

Please visit our website at www.lamplight.net. Please tell us if this book has made a difference in your life. We would like to hear from you. Please send us an email at lamplightmin@yahoo.com or write to us at Lamplight Ministries, Inc., P.O. Box 1307, Dunedin, FL, 34697.

You also can request our free monthly newsletter by mail or email. We would like to stay in touch with you with our newsletter. You can see updates on forthcoming books and pray for us as we pray for you. You also can receive a daily devotional from a set of our Scripture Meditation Cards as well as Judy's monthly Health in a Nutshell bulletin. You can download the first chapter of each of our books.

Our books that have been translated into other languages are downloadable for free as well. Our mission is to help you get into the Word of God and to help you get the Word of God into yourself.

Dear heavenly Father, we pray Your blessing on our reader as he or she experiences You through Your Word, the Bible, on the pages of this book. Father, we pray that You will quicken the reader's spirit to receive Your message for him or her. We pray that he or she will walk with You closely every day. Father, please reveal Yourself to the reader in a glorious way. In Jesus' name, we pray. Amen.

Jack and Judy Hartman

 Lamplight Ministries Inc.

PO Box 1307

Dunedin, Florida 34697-2921

Telephone: 1-800-540-1597

FAX: 1-727-784-2980

Website: lamplight.net

Email: lamplightmin@yahoo.com

Facebook: facebook.com/jackandjudylamplight

Twitter: twitter.com/lamplightmin

Blog: lamplightmin.wordpress.com

Ebooks: Go to smashwords.com. Type in "Jack Hartman"

ISBN: 978-0-915445-60-8

Library of Congress Control Number: 2015955990

Dedication

We are pleased to dedicate this book to evangelist Mary Sarindhorn of Bangkok, Thailand. In her first email to us approximately ten years ago, Mary said, "I was given your book *Trust God For Your Finances* by a friend of mine. As soon as I started reading, I could not put the book down. I have done exactly what you recommended in this book."

In another email Mary said "I have helped my friend translate *Trust God For Your Finances* into Thai. I intended to make about 50 or 60 photocopies of this translation to distribute to my friends. After my pastor read the translation he asked for 700 copies to distribute at the special yearly conference for pastors. My immediate thought was that I could not do this, but he urged me to pray and try my best. Surprisingly, it worked out. Thank God. More than 1,000 people attended the conference. We distributed 700 copies to only the pastors, elders and deacons who really wanted the book. After the conference we had so many calls that another 2,000 copies were printed. Thank you, Mr. Hartman for this book which is helping so many Thai Christians."

Mary has quoted from our books when she speaks in her evangelical conferences. Mary has quoted from our books in Thailand, the Philippines, Indonesia and Columbia. Mary, we thank the Lord for our relationship. We are honored and privileged to dedicate this book to you. We look forward to continued correspondence with you in the future.

Table of Contents

Introduction

If Jesus Christ is your Savior, you can be certain that the same God Who created you lives in your heart. We will study several passages of Scripture pertaining to this magnificent spiritual truth. We also will study Scripture that explains that Jesus Christ and the Holy Spirit also live in the heart of every person who has received Jesus Christ as his or her Savior.

If you are not absolutely certain that Jesus Christ is your Savior, we urge you to stop reading now. Go to the Appendix at the end of this book. Read this Appendix carefully. Receive Jesus Christ as your Savior. Eternal life in heaven begins the moment you believe.

God does not live in the hearts of unbelievers. The unbelief of these people blocks them from having God Who created them living in their hearts. "...your iniquities have made a separation between you and your God, and your sins have hidden His face from you..." (Isaiah 59:2)

We pray that you will carefully study and meditate on the Scripture references in this book. We believe that these promises of God's indwelling presence will transform the life of every person who will obey God's specific instructions to meditate day and night on this Scripture (see Joshua 1:8 and Psalm 1:2-3).

We now use *The Amplified Bible* exclusively in our books. I (Jack) have been using *The Amplified Bible* since 1975. At that time only *The Amplified New Testament* was available. I bought this version of the Bible when I saw it in a Christian bookstore because of an inscription from Dr. Billy Graham on the cover. Dr. Graham said, "This is the best Study Testament on the market. It is a magnificent translation. I use it constantly."

The Amplified Bible is the result of the study of a group of Bible scholars who spent a total of more than 20,000 hours amplifying the Bible. They believe that traditional word-by-word translation often fails to reveal the shades of meaning that are part of the original Greek, Hebrew and Aramaic biblical texts.

Their amplification of the original text uses brackets for words that clarify the meaning and parentheses for words that contain additional phrases included in the original language. Through this amplification the reader will gain a better understanding of what Hebrew and Greek listeners instinctively understood.

We would like to give you a specific example of why we use *The Amplified Bible* exclusively:

- "I can do all things through Christ which strengtheneth me." (Philippians 4:13, *The King James Version*)

- "I can do all this through him who gives me strength." (Philippians 4:13, *The New International Version*)

- "I have strength for all things in Christ Who empowers me [I am ready for anything and equal to anything through Him Who infuses inner strength

into me; I am self-sufficient in Christ's sufficiency]."
(Philippians 4:13, *The Amplified Bible*)

Please note the significant amplification of the original Greek in *The Amplified Bible*. If you make the decision to meditate on Philippians 4:13, you will find that there is much more depth of meaning in *The Amplified Bible* version of this verse.

We recommend that you first read through this book completely. Enjoy God's continued teaching regarding His indwelling presence in your heart.

Then read through the book a second time and highlight or underline all Scripture references and our explanation of this Scripture that is especially meaningful to you. Write notes in the margin or at the top or bottom of each page. If you do, you then will be able to meditate on the specific passages of Scripture that you have identified as being important to you.

We blend together our explanations of Scripture. We thank God for the high privilege of dividing His Word, each of us bringing different expertise to create a final book for you. Imagine a husband and wife, each with a bedroom/office at home, working together every day with different viewpoints that God brings together harmoniously. We are very grateful that God has used us in this way since 1991.

We explain each passage of Scripture in simple and easy-to-understand language. We pray that the scriptural contents of this book and our explanation of this Scripture will help you to learn valuable scriptural truths pertaining to the undeniable truth that God the Father, Jesus Christ and the Holy Spirit live in *your* heart if Jesus Christ is your Savior.

Chapter 1

Your Father Lives in Your Heart

God's ways are much higher and very different from the ways of human beings (see Isaiah 55:8-9). Do not limit God by the limitations of your human logic and understanding. We will begin by studying the theme verse of Scripture for this book. "One God and Father of [us] all, Who is above all [Sovereign over all], pervading all and [living] in [us] all." (Ephesians 4:6)

God is your Father if Jesus Christ is your Savior. God lives "above all" in heaven where He sits on His throne (see Zechariah 6:13). The amplification says that God is "Sovereign over all." The word "sovereign" in this context means that God rules over everyone and everything in the entire universe (see I Chronicles 29:11-12).

We then are told that God "pervades" everything. The word "pervade" means to be spread out. God is above all in heaven. He is spread out throughout the entire universe. Ephesians 4:6 concludes by telling us that God lives in the heart of His children (those who have received Jesus Christ into their hearts).

God is omnipresent. Stuart Hamblen's great song "How Big Is God?" contains the following words: "He is big enough to rule this mighty universe, yet small enough to live within my heart."

God is not limited to being in one place. He can be and is in an infinite number of places at the same time. "...Do not I fill heaven and earth? says the Lord." (Jeremiah 23:24)

God *fills* heaven and earth. His mighty presence is everywhere. "Anyone who confesses (acknowledges, owns) that Jesus is the Son of God, God abides (lives, makes His home) in him and he [abides, lives, makes his home] in God." (I John 4:15)

The word "anyone" at the beginning of this verse is all-inclusive. *Every* person who has received Jesus Christ as his or her Savior can be certain that God "abides, lives, makes His home in him." If Jesus Christ is your Savior, the Creator of the universe lives in *your* heart. God is your Father. You are His beloved child. "...in Christ Jesus you are all sons of God through faith." (Galatians 3:26)

The words "through faith" at the end of this verse instruct you to *believe* that God truly *is* your Father. The Holy Spirit Who lives in the heart of every person who has received Jesus Christ as his or her Savior will confirm this great spiritual truth. "The Spirit Himself [thus] testifies together with our own spirit, [assuring us] that we are children of God." (Romans 8:16)

Every person who receives Jesus Christ as his or her Savior receives the Holy Spirit. "...because you [really] are [His] sons, God has sent the [Holy] Spirit of His

Son into our hearts, crying, Abba (Father)! Father!" (Galatians 4:6)

God has sent the Holy Spirit to live in your heart to assure you that you are God's child and that God truly is your Father. The word "Abba" means father. "...to as many as did receive and welcome Him, He gave the authority (power, privilege, right) to become the children of God, that is, to those who believe in (adhere to, trust in, and rely on) His name—who owe their birth neither to bloods nor to the will of the flesh [that of physical impulse] nor to the will of man [that of a natural father], but to God. [They are born of God!]" (John 1:12-13)

You were born physically when you emerged from your mother's womb. You are born again spiritually when you receive Jesus Christ as your Savior. You are born of God at that time. God Himself becomes your Father. "...you are no longer outsiders (exiles, migrants, and aliens, excluded from the rights of citizens), but you now share citizenship with the saints (God's own people, consecrated and set apart for Himself); and you belong to God's [own] household." (Ephesians 2:19)

Unbelievers are outsiders. They are prohibited from being members of the family of God. If Jesus Christ is your Savior, you "belong to God's own household." God always emphasizes through repetition. His Word repeatedly tells you that He is your Father. God said, "...I will be a Father to you, and you shall be My sons and daughters...." (II Corinthians 6:18)

If Jesus Christ is your Savior, you can be *certain* that the same God Who created you is your Father. "See what [an incredible] quality of love the Father has given (shown, bestowed on) us, that we should [be permitted to] be named and called and counted the children of God! And so we are!..." (I John 3:1)

God's love for each of us is so incredible that all Christians are God's children. Do *not* look at God as being far away from you. God could not be closer to you. He said, "Am I a God at hand, says the Lord, and not a God afar off?" (Jeremiah 23:23)

God is omnipresent. He lives in heaven. He also lives in your heart if Jesus Christ is your Savior. He wants you to be certain that He is not far away. He lives inside of you. "...He is not far from each one of us. For in Him we live and move and have our being..." (Acts 17:27-28)

God wants you to "live and move and have your being" in Him. He wants you to be *so* certain that He is your Father and that He lives in your heart that every aspect of your life revolves around your absolute certainty of His indwelling presence.

Do not put anyone or anything ahead of God. Do not put members of your family ahead of God (see Matthew 10:37). Do not put your occupation ahead of God. Focus every aspect of your life on your absolute certainty that God *is* your Father and that He *does* live in your heart.

Unfortunately, many Christians look at God as a distant God. God seems to be far away from them. Do not make the mistake of looking at God as a far-away God. This chapter contains several verses of Scripture confirming that God could not be closer to you. Enjoy your loving Father 24 hours a day throughout every day of your life.

In this first chapter we have studied several verses of Scripture that assure you that, if Jesus Christ is your Savior, God is your Father and He lives in your heart. In the next chapter we will study Scripture that explains the supernatural power of God. If Jesus Christ is your Savior, the supernatural power of Almighty God, the Creator and the Ruler of the entire universe, lives *within you.*

Chapter 2

The Supernatural Power of God Is within You

In this chapter we will study Scripture that will explain how God's supernatural power can and will help you *if* you know what the Bible instructs you to do to receive His power. Jesus Christ is our example in every area of our lives. Jesus was very much aware of the supernatural power of God within Him throughout His earthly ministry. He said, "...the Father Who lives continually in Me does the (His) works (His own miracles, deeds of power)." (John 14:10)

Jesus Christ was equal to God and had supernatural power when He was in heaven (see Philippians 2:5-8). However, Jesus chose to set aside this supernatural power when He came to earth as a human being. Throughout His earthly ministry Jesus depended totally on God's power in Him and through Him just as you can do (see John 5:19).

The *same* Father God Who lived in the heart of Jesus at that time lives in your heart today if Jesus Christ is your Savior. God's supernatural power can and will work in you and through you just as His power worked in and through His beloved Son during His earthly ministry.

Live every day of your life with a continual consciousness that *you* have the same supernatural power within you that created all of the planets and galaxies in the universe. You have supernatural power within you that is greater than nuclear power or any other power on earth. "The Lord your God is in the midst of you, a Mighty One..." (Zephaniah 3:17)

Do not fear anyone or anything on earth. Identify continually with God living in your heart and with His supernatural power. God is not afraid of anyone or anything. You have every right to be afraid if you are depending on your limited human abilities (see Isaiah 2:22, Galatians 3:3 and Philippians 2:13).

God does *not* require you to depend on your human abilities. Live with a constant awareness that the same God Who created heaven and earth lives in your heart. The prophet Jeremiah said, "...Behold, You have made the heavens and the earth by Your great power and by Your outstretched arm! There is nothing too hard or too wonderful for You." (Jeremiah 32:17)

No problem that you will ever face, no matter how difficult this problem may seem, is too difficult for Almighty God Who lives within you. The Bible speaks of God "Who made [the constellations] the Bear, Orion, and the [loose cluster] Pleiades, and the [vast starry] spaces of the south; Who does great things past finding out, yes, marvelous things without number." (Job 9:9-10)

The same God Who created earth, the moon, the stars and all of the planets and galaxies lives in your heart if Jesus Christ is your Savior. He is able to do great things in you, through you and for you that are beyond the limitations of your human comprehension. "...You reign over all. In Your hands are power and might; in Your hands it is to make great and to give strength to all." (I Chronicles 29:12)

When this verse says that God will "give strength to all," the word "all" includes you. Your Father Who lives in your heart places His supernatural strength and power within you when you receive Jesus Christ as your Savior.

How great and mighty and strong and powerful is God? The Bible speaks of "...the immeasurable and unlimited and surpassing greatness of His power in and for us who believe, as demonstrated in the working of His mighty strength, which He exerted in Christ when He raised Him from the dead and seated Him at His [own] right hand in the heavenly [places]." (Ephesians 1:19-20)

God's supernatural power is "immeasurable and unlimited." His power surpasses anything you could even begin to comprehend with the limitations of your human understanding. God is *so* powerful that He was able to raise Jesus Christ from the dead and to seat Him at His right hand in heaven.

Astronomers know that there are trillions of stars in the universe. There are so many stars that no human being can even begin to count the exact number of stars. God Who lives in *your* heart not only knows the exact number of stars He created, but He also has a name for every one of the trillions of stars. "He determines and counts the number of the stars; He calls them all by their names. Great is our Lord and of great power; His understanding is inexhaustible and boundless." (Psalm 147:4-5)

Problems that seem to be very complicated to you are not difficult for God to solve because "His understanding is inexhaustible and boundless." When you face a problem that seems to have no solution, God always can see a way out. Jesus Christ said, "...With men this is impossible, but all things are possible with God." (Matthew 19:26)

Please note the words "all things" in this verse. These words include *every* problem you will ever face, no matter how difficult this problem might seem to you.

God is omnipresent. He also is omniscient. There is nothing in the entire universe that He does not understand completely. The psalmist David spoke of God's omniscience when he said, "O Lord, you have searched me [thoroughly] and have known me. You know my downsitting and my uprising; You understand my thought afar off. You sift and search out my path and my lying down, and You are acquainted with all my ways. For there is not a word in my tongue [still unuttered], but, behold, O Lord, You know it altogether." (Psalm 139:1-4)

God knows when you go to sleep each night and when you wake up. He knows every thought of every one of the billions of people in the world. God knows every word that you speak. He even knows what you will say before you speak. If Jesus Christ is your Savior, you have supernatural power at work within you. "...it is God Who is all the while effectually at work in you [energizing and creating in you the power and desire], both to will and to work for His good pleasure and satisfaction and delight." (Philippians 2:13)

Your Father loves you with an incredible love that is beyond the limitations of your human understanding (see Isaiah 54:10). He is with you at all times. He will keep you safe. "...The beloved of the Lord shall dwell in safety by Him; He covers him all the day long, and makes His dwelling between his shoulders." (Deuteronomy 33:12)

God Who lives in your heart is watching over you all day long every day of your life. He will help you to the degree that you focus on His indwelling presence and trust in His supernatural power.

God will not always use His power instantly when you face adversity. Your faith in Him is necessary to release His supernatural power on your behalf. The Bible speaks of "...those who through faith (by their leaning of the entire personality on God in Christ in absolute trust and confidence in His power, wisdom, and goodness) and by practice of patient endurance and waiting are [now] inheriting the promises." (Hebrews 6:12)

God's supernatural power will be released in your life to the degree that you lean completely on Him "with absolute trust and confidence in His power, wisdom, and goodness." You will inherit God's promises to the degree that you add "patient endurance and waiting" to your faith in God.

Focus continually on Scripture pertaining to God's indwelling presence, His supernatural power and His promises to help you and strengthen you when you face severe adversity. Keep trusting God with unwavering faith in Him for as long as He requires you to persevere in faith.

In this chapter we have studied Scripture pertaining to the omnipotence and omniscience of God and God's promises to release His mighty power in your life. In the next two chapters we will study what the Bible teaches about the supernatural power of Jesus Christ Who lives in your heart and the Holy Spirit Who lives in your heart. The more that you know and understand about the supernatural power that is at work within you, the more certain you will be that you *are* able to live in the resurrection power of Jesus Christ.

Chapter 3

Jesus Christ Lives in Your Heart

In the last chapter we studied Scripture explaining that God is omnipresent. God can sit on His throne in heaven and rule the entire universe and also live in the heart of every Christian throughout the world. Jesus Christ *also* is omnipresent. He can sit on His throne in heaven next to God and also live in the heart of every Christian in the world. "All who keep His commandments [who obey His orders and follow His plan, live and continue to live, to stay and] abide in Him, and He in them. [They let Christ be a home to them and they are the home of Christ.]..." (I John 3:24)

You are instructed to "abide" in Jesus Christ as He abides in you. You abide in Christ to the degree that you obey God's instructions and focus on His indwelling presence. The more conscious you are of God's indwelling presence, the more you will know that Jesus Christ also lives in your heart. "May Christ through your faith [actually] dwell (settle down, abide, make His permanent home) in your hearts!..." (Ephesians 3:17)

Please note the words "through your faith" in this verse. Do you have absolute faith that Jesus Christ lives in your heart because the holy Scriptures say that He does? Your faith is the determining factor pertaining to the indwelling presence of Jesus Christ.

The final amplification in this verse says that Jesus Christ makes His "permanent home" in your heart. The word "permanent" means lasting and unchanging. Jesus Christ will live in your heart throughout the remainder of your life. Jesus said, "...behold, I am with you all the days (perpetually, uniformly, and on every occasion), to the [very] close and consummation of the age...." (Matthew 28:20)

The amplification in this verse says that Jesus Christ is with you "on every occasion." No matter what you do or where you go, Jesus wants you to have absolute certainty that He lives in your heart and that He is always with you. He promises that He will be with you until the end of time.

The following words that Jesus spoke to His disciples many years ago are His words to you today. Jesus said, "...My [own] peace I now give and bequeath to you. Not as the world gives do I give to you. Do not let your hearts be troubled, neither let them be afraid. [Stop allowing yourselves to be agitated and disturbed; and do not permit yourselves to be fearful and intimidated and cowardly and unsettled.]" (John 14:27)

Jesus has given *you* His supernatural peace. Refuse to allow yourself to be afraid of anything. Why would you ever be afraid of anything if you are absolutely certain that the victorious Jesus Christ lives in your heart? Jesus said, "...In the world you have tribulation and trials and distress and frustration; but be of good cheer [take courage; be confident, certain, undaunted]!

For I have overcome the world. [I have deprived it of power to harm you and have conquered it for you.]" (John 16:33)

When Jesus Christ victoriously rose from death, He won a victory over every problem you will ever face. The amplification at the end of this verse says that He has deprived any problem in the world from being able to harm you because He has conquered it for you.

The more that you study and meditate on the Scripture references in this chapter, the more certain you will be that the victorious Jesus Christ really does live in your heart. "...Do you not yourselves realize and know [thoroughly by an ever-increasing experience] that Jesus Christ is in you...?" (II Corinthians 13:5)

The apostle Paul was absolutely certain that Jesus Christ lived in his heart. Paul had been beaten, tortured, stoned and shipwrecked, but he persevered throughout all adversity because of his absolute faith that Jesus Christ lived in his heart. Paul said, "For me to live is Christ [His life in me]..." (Philippians 1:21)

Paul died to himself. Jesus Christ was his entire life. Paul said, "I have been crucified with Christ [in Him I have shared His crucifixion]; it is no longer I who live, but Christ (the Messiah) lives in me; and the life I now live in the body I live by faith in (by adherence to and reliance on and complete trust in) the Son of God, Who loved me and gave Himself up for me." (Galatians 2:20)

The amplification at the beginning of this verse says that Paul "shared" in the crucifixion of Christ. Paul went on to say that he no longer was living his life for himself. Jesus Christ Who lived in his heart was in control. Paul had absolute faith in Christ.

Follow Paul's example. Live your life with absolute and complete trust in the indwelling Jesus Christ Who gave His life for you. Keep Jesus in first place in your life at all times. Have a continual consciousness of the indwelling presence of the victorious Jesus Christ Who gave His life for you and won a total victory over every problem you will ever face. Jesus said, "He who loves [and takes more pleasure in] father or mother more than [in] Me is not worthy of Me; and he who loves [and takes more pleasure in] son or daughter more than [in] Me is not worthy of Me." (Matthew 10:37)

These words that Jesus spoke to His disciples many years ago are His words to you. Love Jesus first. Then you will love your parents, your spouse and your children with a greater love than you ever thought possible.

In the last two chapters we have studied Scripture assuring you that Father God lives in your heart and that Jesus Christ lives in your heart. In the next chapter we will carefully study what the Bible teaches about the third person of the holy Trinity, the Holy Spirit, Who *also* lives in your heart.

Chapter 4

The Holy Spirit Lives in Your Heart

At the Last Supper Jesus began to prepare His disciples for what their lives would be like after He died, rose from the dead and ascended into heaven. Jesus said, "...I will ask the Father, and He will give you another Comforter (Counselor, Helper, Intercessor, Advocate, Strengthener, and Standby), that He may remain with you forever—the Spirit of Truth, Whom the world cannot receive (welcome, take to its heart), because it does not see Him or know and recognize Him. But you know and recognize Him, for He lives with you [constantly] and will be in you." (John 14:16-17)

Jesus told His disciples that He no longer would be with them in the flesh after He ascended into heaven. He told them that God would provide "another Comforter" for them even though He no longer would be there to comfort and help them. This Comforter is the Holy Spirit.

The amplification in this verse explains the many things that the Holy Spirit would do to help the disciples. These words that Jesus spoke to His disciples also are His words to you today in regard to what the Holy Spirit will do in your life.

The Holy Spirit comes into your heart the moment you believe and receive Jesus Christ as your Savior. He is your Helper. If you trust Him completely, He will help you with the problems you face. He wants you to be certain that He *will* help you whenever you need help.

The Holy Spirit is your Intercessor. He represents you to God. He intercedes for you when you pray to God.

The Holy Spirit is your Advocate. An advocate is someone who pleads for another person. A lawyer is an example of an advocate. The Holy Spirit pleads to God on your behalf.

The Holy Spirit is your Strengthener. When you are weak, He will strengthen you with His supernatural strength, power and ability.

The Holy Spirit is your Standby. He stands by you throughout every minute of every hour of every day of your life. He is with you at all times, no matter what challenges you face.

Unbelievers cannot receive the Holy Spirit. Unbelievers live worldly lives that are dictated by their senses. Only Christians who have received Jesus Christ as their Savior receive the Holy Spirit.

Study and meditate on the Scripture references in this chapter. You did not do anything to earn the Holy Spirit. You do not deserve to have the Holy Spirit living within you. God gave you the Holy Spirit as His *gift* to you. "Do you not know that your body is the temple (the very sanctuary) of the Holy Spirit Who lives within you, Whom you have received [as a Gift] from God? You are not your own..." (I Corinthians 6:19)

In previous chapters we explained that God is omnipresent. He is able to be in an infinite number of places at the same time. He can sit on His throne in heaven and live in the heart of every Christian believer throughout the world. Jesus Christ also is omnipresent. He sits on a throne next to God in heaven. He also lives in the heart of every Christian throughout the world. The Holy Spirit is omnipresent. "...God's Spirit has His permanent dwelling in you [to be at home in you, collectively as a church and also individually]..." (I Corinthians 3:16)

The Holy Spirit lives collectively in the hearts of all Christians everywhere. He also lives individually in your heart. The Holy Spirit has His "permanent dwelling" in your heart. God put the Holy Spirit in your heart to guide you and to help you to understand His Word and obey His instructions. God said, "...I will put my Spirit within you and cause you to walk in My statutes, and you shall heed My ordinances and do them." (Ezekiel 36:27)

Your Father wants you to yield control of your life to the Holy Spirit. He wants you to "...live and move not in the ways of the flesh but in the ways of the Spirit [our lives governed not by the standards and according to the dictates of the flesh, but controlled by the Holy Spirit]." (Romans 8:4)

Unbelievers center their lives around their fleshly desires. God wants you to center your life around "the ways of the Spirit." He wants your life not to be controlled by fleshly desires but to be controlled by the Holy Spirit. "...you are living the life of the Spirit, if the [Holy] Spirit of God [really] dwells within you [directs and controls you]...." (Romans 8:9)

You are living the way that God wants you to live to the degree that you yield control of your life to the Holy Spirit and allow Him to direct and control your life. The more that you turn away from fleshly desires and turn to godly desires, the more you will grow and mature as a Christian. Jesus said, "Whoever finds his [lower] life will lose it [the higher life], and whoever loses his [lower] life on My account will find it [the higher life]." (Matthew 10:39)

Unbelievers and unyielded Christians are focused on their "lower life" – a life of worldly goals and desires. Mature Christians who yield control of their lives to the Holy Spirit experience "the higher life." God progressively reveals life to them from His perspective. "...walk and live [habitually] in the [Holy] Spirit [responsive to and controlled and guided by the Spirit]; then you will certainly not gratify the cravings and desires of the flesh (of human nature without God)." (Galatians 5:16)

Please note the word "habitually" in the first amplification in this verse. Surrender control of your life to the Holy Spirit. We have just studied three verses of Scripture (Romans 8:4 and 9 and Galatians 5:8) that instruct you to be controlled by the Holy Spirit. Gladly yield control of your life to the Holy Spirit. Allow Him to guide you continually. The more that you do this, the more you will live the way God wants you to live.

Chapter 5

The Kingdom of God Is within You

In the last chapter we studied John 14:16-17 where you are told that the Holy Spirit will help you and strengthen you. We studied additional Scripture that instructs you to surrender control of your life to the Holy Spirit. If you truly believe that the Holy Spirit will help you and strengthen you and if you do surrender control of your life to the Holy Spirit, you will *not* be afraid when you face severe adversity. God said, "...My Spirit stands and abides in the midst of you; fear not." (Haggai 2:5)

In addition to the Holy Spirit helping you when you face adversity, you can be certain that Jesus Christ Who lives in your heart knows exactly what you are experiencing. He also will help you. "...because He Himself [in His humanity] has suffered in being tempted (tested and tried), He is able [immediately] to run to the cry of (assist, relieve) those who are being tempted and tested and tried [and who therefore are being exposed to suffering]." (Hebrews 2:18)

Please note the words "in His humanity" in the first amplification in this verse. Jesus Christ came to earth as a human being. He trusted completely in His Father.

Because of what Jesus experienced in His humanity during His earthly ministry, He understands exactly what you are going through in your humanity. Because of this understanding, He is able to help you whenever you are being "tempted and tested and tried."

Trust Jesus Christ Who lives in your heart to help you. Trust the Holy Spirit Who lives in your heart to help you. Trust the same God Who created heaven and earth and lives in your heart to help you. Be like the psalmist who said, "My help comes from the Lord, Who made heaven and earth." (Psalm 121:2)

The same God Who helped the psalmist will help you if you have absolute faith in the complete reliability of every promise in His Word (see Numbers 23:19, Joshua 23:14, Jeremiah 1:12, I Corinthians 1:9, II Corinthians 1:20 and Hebrews 6:18). Focus continually on the indwelling presence of God, Jesus Christ and the Holy Spirit. "...you are in Him, made full and having come to fullness of life [in Christ you too are filled with the Godhead—Father, Son and Holy Spirit—and reach full spiritual stature]...." (Colossians 2:10)

If Jesus Christ is your Savior, you are "filled with the Godhead – Father, Son and Holy Spirit." You will "reach full spiritual stature" if you are absolutely certain that Father God, Jesus Christ and the Holy Spirit live in your heart. Place all of your trust and confidence in Father, Son and Holy Spirit to live in you and through you and to solve severe problems that you cannot solve with the limitations of your human ability. Jesus said,

"...the kingdom of God is within you [in your hearts] and among you [surrounding you]." (Luke 17:21)

The kingdom of God is not limited to heaven. The kingdom of God is within the heart of every believer. When you receive Jesus Christ as your Savior, you are connected to God. You are spiritually plugged into the kingdom of God within your heart.

In the last five chapters we have studied many Scripture references about God, Jesus Christ and the Holy Spirit living inside of you. The New Testament speaks primarily of God *in* you. The Old Testament speaks often of God being *with* you. In the next two chapters we will carefully study what the Bible teaches about God being with you at all times.

Chapter 6

God Is Always with You

If you are a Christian, you are never alone. God promises that He will be with you whenever you face adversity. God promises that He will bring you safely through this adversity. God said, "He shall call upon Me, and I will answer him; I will be with him in trouble, I will deliver him..." (Psalm 91:15)

God repeatedly promises that He will be with you when you face adversity. God said, "When you pass through the waters, I will be with you, and through the rivers, they will not overwhelm you. When you walk through the fire, you will not be burned or scorched, nor will the flame kindle upon you." (Isaiah 43:2)

Please note that the word "through" is used *three times* in this verse of Scripture. Your Father promises to bring you safely *through* whatever problems you face. Persevere in your faith in God. Absolutely refuse to give up. This promise that God made to the Israelites many years ago also is God's promise to you today.

When you face adversity, refuse to focus on the adversity. Focus instead on the undeniable truth that the same God Who created you is with you in this adversity. Meditate continually on God's promises to bring you safely through whatever problems you face. "The strong spirit of a man sustains him in bodily pain or trouble..." (Proverbs 18:14)

The words "strong spirit" refer to your faith in God. Meditate continually on these promises that God is with you when you are in trouble and that He will bring you through all adversity. God said, "...call on Me in the day of trouble; I will deliver you..." (Psalm 50:15)

This book is filled with promises that God lives in your heart if Jesus Christ is your Savior. He is with you throughout every minute of every hour of every day. He will bring you safely through all adversity. "God is our Refuge and Strength [mighty and impenetrable to temptation], a very present and well-proved help in trouble. Therefore we will not fear..." (Psalm 46:1-2)

Your Father promises that He will give you supernatural strength whenever you are in trouble. Do not be afraid. Have absolute faith that God *will* help you. "...with God nothing is ever impossible and no word from God shall be without power or impossible of fulfillment." (Luke 1:37)

The word "nothing" in this verse applies to whatever problem you face. If you know that God is with you and that He can solve every problem, no matter how difficult any problem may seem to you, absolutely refuse to give up. "Have not I commanded you? Be strong, vigorous, and very courageous. Be not afraid, neither be dismayed, for the Lord your God is with you wherever you go." (Joshua 1:9)

These words that God spoke to Joshua when he succeeded Moses as the leader of Israel also are God's words to you today. God *commands* you not to be afraid because of your certainty that He is with you wherever you go.

God always emphasizes through repetition. He repeatedly instructs you not to be afraid because He is with you. God said, "Fear not [there is nothing to fear], for I am with you; do not look around you in terror and be dismayed, for I am your God. I will strengthen and harden you to difficulties, yes, I will help you; yes, I will hold you up and retain you with My [victorious] right hand of rightness and justice." (Isaiah 41:10)

Once again God tells you not to be afraid because He is with you. He will strengthen you. He will help you. "The Lord will give [unyielding and impenetrable] strength to His people..." (Psalm 29:11)

The amplification in this verse speaks of "unyielding and impenetrable strength." God promises to give you supernatural strength that is so strong that it will not yield to anything. Nothing can penetrate the supernatural strength that God will give you. "...be strong in the Lord [be empowered through your union with Him]; draw your strength from Him [that strength which His boundless might provides]." (Ephesians 6:10)

Please note the words "through your union with Him" in the first amplification in this verse. Stay close to God. Focus continually on His indwelling presence.

The apostle Paul faced a great deal of adversity in his life. Paul said, "...I am well pleased and take pleasure in infirmities, insults, hardships, persecutions, perplexities and distresses; for when I am weak [in human strength], then am I [truly] strong (able, powerful in divine strength)." (II Corinthians 12:10)

God's ways are very different and very much higher than the ways of human beings (see Isaiah 55:8-9). Your Father instructs you to be "well-pleased and take pleasure" when you face adversity. *Why* would you be pleased when you face severe problems? Paul went on to explain that he was pleased that God would give him His supernatural strength when he was weak in human strength.

The following words that Moses spoke to the Israelites when they faced a mighty Egyptian army are God's words to you today. "Be strong, courageous, and firm; fear not nor be in terror before them, for it is the Lord your God Who goes with you; He will not fail you or forsake you." (Deuteronomy 31:6)

Refuse to yield to any problem you face, no matter how powerful it is. Your Father goes with you. He promises that He will never fail you or forsake you. God said, "...behold, I am with you and will keep (watch over you with care, take notice of) you wherever you may go." (Genesis 28:15)

You can be certain that your Father is with you at all times. He assures you that He is watching over you. Be like the psalmist who said, "...I am continually with You; You do hold my right hand. You will guide me with Your counsel..." (Psalm 73:23-24)

Think back to when you were a little child. Did you feel secure when one of your parents was holding your hand? You can be secure today because you know that your heavenly Father is "continually with you" and that He is holding your hand.

This chapter is filled with promises that God will help you when you face adversity. In the next chapter we will study additional promises that also assure you that God is with you when you face adversity and that He will bring you through every problem you face.

Chapter 7

God Will Fight for You

Your Father is with you at all times. You can trust Him completely to fight battles that you cannot win with your limited human abilities. "...the Lord your God is He Who goes with you to fight for you against your enemies...." (Deuteronomy 20:4)

These words that Moses spoke to the Israelites are God's words to you today. King Hezekiah, the king of Judah, spoke similar words to his followers when they faced a mighty army that was overwhelming in its power. He said, "...with us is the Lord our God to help us and to fight our battles...." (II Chronicles 32:8)

God always emphasizes through repetition. When you see the same principle being stated in two or more Scripture references, you can be certain that God is emphasizing what He is telling you. Your Father has just told you twice that He *is* with you and that He *will* fight your battles for you.

Refuse to be overwhelmed when you face a difficult challenge. Meditate on these passages of Scripture. Know that God is with you. He will help you. "Let us then fearlessly and confidently and boldly draw near to the throne of grace (the throne of God's unmerited favor to us sinners), that we may receive mercy [for our failures] and find grace to help in good time for every need [appropriate help and well-timed help, coming just when we need it]." (Hebrews 4:16)

Once again you are instructed not to be afraid. Trust God completely. Humble yourself before Him. Draw near to His throne of grace. He promises to give you mercy and grace. This verse and the amplification promise that God will help you with "every need, appropriate help and well-timed help coming just when you need it." Trust God to meet *every* need that you have (see Psalms 23:1, 14:9-10 and 84:11, Romans 8:32, Philippians 4:19 and II Peter 1:3). Trust His perfect timing (see Psalm 104:19, Luke 1:20 and James 5:7-8).

When King Jehoshaphat and the Israelites faced a vastly superior army, God did not want them to be afraid. He told them that He would fight the battle for them. The following words that God spoke to King Jehoshaphat are God's words to you today. "...The Lord says this to you: Be not afraid or dismayed at this great multitude; for the battle is not yours, but God's." (II Chronicles 20:15)

Once again you are instructed *not* to be afraid when you face a formidable challenge. No matter how difficult any problem may be, you can be certain that God is with you and that He will fight the battle for you. "The Lord will fight for you, and you shall hold your peace and remain at rest." (Exodus 14:14)

Moses spoke these words to his followers when they were pursued by a large Egyptian army. Moses assured the Israelites that the Lord would fight for them. He did not want them to be afraid. He instructed them to rest in God.

God honored the faith of the Israelites. Even though the Israelites were pursued by a large army behind them and they faced high and impassable mountains to the right and left and the Red Sea before them, God made a way. "Then Moses stretched out his hand over the sea, and the Lord caused the sea to go back by a strong east wind all that night and made the sea dry land; and the waters were divided. And the Israelites went into the midst of the sea on dry ground, the waters being a wall to them on their right hand and on their left." (Exodus 14:21-22)

God supernaturally caused the Red Sea to be parted so there would be a passage of dry land where the Israelites could go through. God told Moses exactly what to do when the Egyptian army attempted to follow. "Then the Lord said to Moses, Stretch out your hand over the sea, that the waters may come again upon the Egyptians, upon their chariots and horsemen." (Exodus 14:26)

Moses obeyed God's instructions. When the Egyptians attempted to follow the Israelites, the water returned and destroyed the formidable Egyptian army. "So Moses stretched forth his hand over the sea, and the sea returned to its strength and normal flow when the morning appeared; and the Egyptians fled into it [being met by it]; and the Lord overthrew the Egyptians and shook them off into the midst of the sea. The waters returned and covered the chariots, the horsemen, and all the host of Pharaoh that pursued them; not even one of them remained." (Exodus 14:27-28)

This marvelous story of the help that God gave to the Israelites many years ago is a perfect example of the help that your Father will give you today. Focus on His indwelling presence. Rest in Him, absolutely refusing to be upset by the severity of any obstacle you face. "...the Lord said, My Presence shall go with you, and I will give you rest." (Exodus 33:14)

These words that God spoke to Moses many years ago are God's words to you today. Focus continually on God's indwelling presence. Know that He is with you. Rest in Him. Refuse to be overwhelmed by the severity of any problem you face. "...the Lord has given you rest from your sorrow and pain and from your trouble and unrest..." (Isaiah 14:3)

God wants you to know that He is with you at all times. He wants you to be certain that He will bring you safely through whatever problem you face *if* you will rest in Him. "...he who has once entered [God's] rest also has ceased from [the weariness and pain] of human labors..." (Hebrews 4:10)

This verse and the amplification instruct you to cease from trying to solve difficult problems with your limited human abilities. Do not struggle and strain. Do not try to make things happen. Enter into God's rest. Trust your Father within you completely to do in you, for you and through you what you cannot do yourself.

Chapter 8

Turn Away from the World

The first five chapters of this book were filled with encouraging Scripture references. The holy Scriptures assure you that, if Jesus Christ is your Savior, the same God Who created you lives in your heart. The victorious Jesus Christ lives in your heart. The Holy Spirit lives in your heart.

We devoted Chapters 6 and 7 to what the Bible teaches about God being *with* you. If God lives in you, He obviously is with you at all times. Your Father has given you many promises telling of the blessings that He will give you because He is continually with you.

In this chapter we will study Scripture that will encourage you to turn away from trusting in your human abilities and from placing all of your trust in worldly sources of security. Place your trust and confidence in the indwelling presence of God the Father, Jesus Christ and the Holy Spirit. God's Word instructs us to "...put no confidence or dependence [on what we are] in the flesh and on outward privileges and physical advantages and external appearances." (Philippians 3:3)

Some Christians are fearful because they think that they need to solve difficult problems with their human abilities. Your Father instructs you to put "no confidence" in your human abilities and in external sources of security. God instructs each of His children to "...keep oneself unspotted and uncontaminated from the world." (James 1:27)

If your life revolves around the indwelling presence of God, you will not be contaminated by anything in the world. Your priorities will be the way God wants them to be. "For all that is in the world—the lust of the flesh [craving for sensual gratification] and the lust of the eyes [greedy longings of the mind] and the pride of life [assurance in one's own resources or in the stability of earthly things]—these do not come from the Father but are from the world [itself]." (I John 2:16)

The second amplification in this verse speaks of "assurance in one's own resources or in the stability of earthly things." Trust God as your only source of security. Turn within yourself for the greatest security in the entire universe – the indwelling presence of Almighty God.

Do not live the way that many religious people live. Their lives do not revolve around the indwelling presence of God. The following words that Jesus Christ spoke about the Pharisees apply to many people today. Jesus said, "These people draw near Me with their mouths and honor Me with their lips, but their hearts hold off and are far away from Me." (Matthew 15:8)

Do not be a person who goes through the motions of being religious without being completely focused on the indwelling presence of Father God, Jesus Christ and the Holy Spirit. The following words that the apostle Paul wrote in his letter to the Colossians many years ago are God's words to you today. Paul, speaking of Jesus Christ, instructed the Colossians to live in such a way that "...He alone in everything and in every respect might occupy the chief place [stand first and be preeminent]." (Colossians 1:18)

Keep the indwelling presence of God first in your life – far ahead of anything in the world. Be like the psalmist who said, "...I have no delight or desire on earth besides You." (Psalm 73:25)

Do not make the mistake that some Christians make of paying mental assent to the truth of the indwelling presence of God, but not centering their lives around Him. What could possibly be more important to you than the great scriptural truth that the Creator of the universe lives in *your* heart if Jesus Christ is your Savior?

We see a good example of this principle in the scriptural story of two sisters named Martha and Mary. Martha invited Jesus to visit in her home. "...Jesus entered a certain village, and a woman named Martha received and welcomed Him into her house." (Luke 10:38)

The following explanation of the different ways that Martha and Mary received Jesus clearly illustrates how Jesus wants you to live today. "...she had a sister named Mary, who seated herself at the Lord's feet and was listening to His teaching. But Martha [overly occupied and too busy] was distracted with much serving; and she came up to Him and said, Lord, is it nothing to You that my sister has left me to serve alone? Tell her then to help me [to lend a hand and do her part along with me]!" (Luke 10:39-40)

Mary focused continually on Jesus. She sat at His feet and listened intently to His teaching. Martha focused on external things. She asked Jesus to tell Mary to help her in her preparation to serve Him.

Mary was concerned only with staying close to Jesus and learning from Him. The following words that Jesus spoke to Martha explain how He wants your relationship with Him to be. "...the Lord replied to her by saying, Martha, Martha, you are anxious and troubled about many things; there is need of only one or but a few things. Mary has chosen the good portion [that which is to her advantage], which shall not be taken away from her." (Luke 10:41-42)

Make the quality decision that you will live the way that Mary lived instead of being preoccupied with seemingly important things in the world the way that Martha did. This book is filled with Scripture references pertaining to the indwelling presence of God, Jesus Christ and the Holy Spirit. Meditate consistently on these Scripture references. Make the decision that your life will revolve continually around the indwelling presence of God instead of revolving around anyone or anything in the world.

Live your life consistently from the inside out, not from the outside in. Center your life around your Father Who lives in your heart, Jesus Christ Who lives in your heart and the Holy Spirit Who lives in your heart.

Chapter 9

Keep God in First Place

Your Father instructs you to focus continually on Him. "...set your mind and heart to seek (inquire of and require as your vital necessity) the Lord your God...." (I Chronicles 22:19)

Please note the words "vital necessity" in the amplification in this verse. Keeping God in first place is not a nice-to-have. Keeping God first at all times is absolutely necessary. Your Father wants your life to revolve around Him. "...[earnestly] remember the Lord and imprint Him [on your minds]..." (Nehemiah 4:14)

When you do something "earnestly," you are very focused on whatever you are doing. You are instructed to "imprint" God on your mind. Think about the indwelling presence of God continually. "Have the roots [of your being] firmly and deeply planted [in Him, fixed and founded in Him], being continually built up in Him, becoming increasingly more confirmed and established in the faith, just as you were taught, and abounding and overflowing in it with thanksgiving." (Colossians 2:7)

Your Father does not want you to have a shallow surface relationship with Him or no relationship at all. He wants your relationship with Him to be deeply rooted. He says that your relationship with Him should be "continually built up." "Seek the Lord [inquire for Him, inquire of Him, and require Him as the foremost necessity of your life]..." (Zephaniah 2:3)

In the amplification of this verse you are instructed to require God as "the foremost necessity of your life." Your Father has specifically instructed you to place your relationship with Him ahead of everything else in your life.

Focus your life around your absolute certainty that the same God Who created you lives in your heart. Have the same focus on the indwelling presence of Jesus Christ and the indwelling presence of the Holy Spirit. The following verse, speaking of Jesus Christ, says, "...abide in (live in, never depart from) Him [being rooted in Him, knit to Him]..." (I John 2:27)

You are instructed to "abide" in Christ. The first amplification instructs you to "never depart" from Him. The second amplification instructs you to be "rooted in Him, knit to Him."

Do these words describe *your* relationship with Jesus Christ? Does every aspect of your life revolve around the indwelling presence of the victorious Jesus Christ Who rose from the dead to give His supernatural victory to you? "...thanks be to God, Who in Christ always leads us in triumph [as trophies of Christ's victory]..." (II Corinthians 2:14)

Thank your Father continually. He has made provision for Jesus Christ to *always* lead you in triumph. Keep God in first place in your life. Keep Jesus Christ first. Keep the Holy Spirit first. Be like the psalmist David who said, "I have set the Lord continually before me; because He is at my right hand, I shall not be moved. Therefore my heart is glad and my glory [my inner self] rejoices; my body too shall rest and confidently dwell in safety." (Psalm 16:8-9)

Please note that David said that he set the Lord *continually* before him. Because of this constant focus on the Lord, David was not moved by any adversity he faced. He rejoiced within himself because he rested in the Lord. He had absolute confidence that the Lord would keep him safe. At a later time David said, "My soul, wait only upon God and silently submit to Him; for my hope and expectation are from Him. He only is my Rock and my Salvation; He is my Defense and my Fortress, I shall not be moved." (Psalm 62:5-6)

Please note David's use of the word "only" two times in this passage of Scripture. David did not look to any other source. He submitted his life to God (see John 12:24-26, Romans 8:9, I Corinthians 6:19-20 and Galatians 2:20, 5:6 and 5:25). Focus your life continually on God Who lives in your heart. "Let your eyes look right on [with fixed purpose], and let your gaze be straight before you. Consider well the path of your feet, and let all your ways be established and ordered aright. Turn not aside to the right hand or to the left; remove your foot from evil." (Proverbs 4:25-27)

This passage of Scripture instructs you to be single-minded. Do not turn to the left or to the right. Keep God in first place at all times. Be continually aware of

His supernatural indwelling presence. Be like the psalmist who said, "My whole being follows hard after You and clings closely to You; Your right hand upholds me." (Psalm 63:8)

The psalmist spoke of his "whole being." Every aspect of his life was focused on God. He clung closely to God at all times. He knew that God would prevent him from falling if he kept Him first and trusted Him completely. "You will guard him and keep him in perfect and constant peace whose mind [both its inclination and its character] is stayed on You, because he commits himself to You, leans on You, and hopes confidently in You." (Isaiah 26:3)

Would you like to be certain that God is guarding you and protecting you at all times? Do you want your Father to keep you in "perfect and constant peace?" God has promised to give you these great blessings if your mind is *stayed* on Him because you are totally and completely committed to Him and because you place all of your hope and confidence in Him.

God has given every person freedom of choice (see Psalm 25:12 and I Corinthians 6:12 and 8:9). He will never force any human being to worship Him. If you choose not to focus on God's indwelling presence, God will allow you to ignore Him. God made the very important decision to live in the heart of *every one* of His children throughout the world. Do not make the mistake that some of God's children make of living their lives with little or no focus on the supernatural indwelling presence of God.

Jesus Christ is your example in every area of life. Throughout His earthly ministry His life revolved continually around God's indwelling presence. He knew that His Father was with Him continually. He kept God in first place at all times.

Do these words describe your life? Are you continually conscious that the God of the universe lives inside of you and that He is with you throughout every minute of every hour of every day of your life? Do you keep Him in first place at all times? Do you trust Him completely?

Some Christians do not know what the Bible teaches about God living in their hearts. Other Christians know this scriptural truth, but they merely pay mental assent to the indwelling presence of God. They are religious, but their lives revolve primarily around personal goals and people and events in the world.

We pray that you will not take the scriptural contents of this book lightly. These Scripture references clearly tell you that the same God Who created everything in the universe lives in *your* heart if Jesus Christ is your Savior. Focus continually on the indwelling presence of God. Keep Him in first place in your life at all times.

Chapter 10

Continually Draw Closer to God

In the last two chapters we discussed the importance of focusing your life on God Who lives in your heart. If you consistently focus your life on the indwelling presence of God, you will have a close and intimate relationship with Him. Jesus Christ shed His precious blood so that you can draw close to God. "...in Christ Jesus, you who once were [so] far away, through (by, in) the blood of Christ have been brought near." (Ephesians 2:13)

All of us are separated from God when we are born. Every person is born as a descendant of Adam. Every person is born with a sin nature derived from Adam and Eve's disobedience to God. People who receive Jesus Christ as their Savior receive a new life. Their inherited sin nature is gone. They have the precious opportunity to continually draw closer to God.

Do not take this great privilege lightly. Learn and obey the specific instructions that your Father has given to you in regard to drawing closer to Him. "...the Son of God has [actually] come to this world and has given us understanding and insight [progressively] to perceive (recognize) and come to know better and more clearly Him Who is true..." (I John 5:20)

Jesus Christ came into this world to give *you* the ability to know God more intimately. The second amplification in this verse instructs you to "progressively" draw closer to God. When you do something progressively, you do whatever you are doing in gradual stages of development. A close and intimate relationship with God is a relationship that will steadily increase over a period of time if you make the decision to consistently focus on drawing closer to God. Do not make the mistake that some Christians make. "...God is great, and we know Him not!..." (Job 36:26)

Many Christians live a religious lifestyle. They go to church one or more times each week. They pray for a few minutes each day. However, their lives revolve around themselves and their personal goals and desires instead of revolving around the indwelling presence of God Who created them. These Christians do not have an intimate relationship with God.

If Jesus Christ is your Savior, you have spiritual power within yourself that is much greater than nuclear power or any other power in the world. If you consistently center your life around the indwelling presence of God and meditate day and night on God's Word, the supernatural power of God will be released in your life. The Bible speaks of "...Him Who, by (in consequence of) the [action of His] power that is at work within us, is able to [carry out His purpose and] do superabundantly, far over and above all that we [dare] ask or think [infinitely beyond our highest prayers, desires, thoughts, hopes, or dreams]." (Ephesians 3:20)

God's power within you is *so* great that He is able to "do superabundantly far over and above all that you dare ask or think." God's power within you is "infinitely beyond your highest prayers, desires, thoughts, hopes, or dreams." Do not miss out on the glorious opportunity to receive this supernatural power that resides within you if Jesus Christ is your Savior.

Be ready to pray immediately for any person who faces a severe problem. We pray immediately whenever we hear a siren letting us know that someone needs God's help, comfort and wisdom. Create the habit of talking to God about everything. Cultivate your relationship with your Father. Cherish Him.

When Jesus Christ becomes your Savior, a new spiritual person is born within you. The Bible refers to this spiritual person as "...the hidden person of the heart..." (I Peter 3:4)

When the Bible speaks of your heart, it does not refer to the organ in your body that pumps blood. It refers to your spiritual heart which is at the center of your being. The hidden person of your heart is the "real you." This spiritual person comes alive within you when you receive Jesus Christ as your Savior.

The hidden person of the heart requires spiritual food just as your body requires natural food. Your body is fed with food that goes into your mouth. The hidden person of the heart is fed with spiritual food that goes into your eyes and your ears as a result of continually feeding the Word of God to yourself through consistent Bible study and Scripture meditation.

Many Christians are spiritually malnourished. They do not feed the Word of God into their minds and their hearts on a regular and consistent basis. They depend on their pastor to do their Bible study for them.

We have spent hundreds of hours finding the Scripture in this book that tells you exactly what to do to constantly draw closer to God Who lives in your heart. Make the quality decision that you will feed this Scripture into your eyes, your ears, your mind and your heart on a regular and consistent basis. Nourish yourself continually with the supernatural spiritual food that God has provided to feed the hidden person of the heart.

Christians who consistently draw closer to God become more and more one with Him. Their lives revolve around His indwelling presence. They turn away from the attractions and diversions in the world. They turn away from personal goals and desires. They follow the example of the psalmist who said, "My inner self thirsts for God, for the living God...." (Psalm 42:2)

The words "inner self" in this verse refer to the hidden person of your heart. Thirst for a close and intimate relationship with the living God. "Come close to God and He will come close to you...." (James 4:8)

You decide how close you will be to God. God did not make you a puppet. He gave you freedom of choice for every decision you make. If you make the quality decision to consistently focus on God's indwelling presence, "He *will* come close to you."

Your loving Father wants to have a close and intimate relationship with each of His children. He wants each of His children to focus his or her life around a constant awareness of His indwelling presence. Develop a humble and teachable attitude. Learn everything that you can about the indwelling presence of God and how to consistently draw closer to Him. "He leads the humble in what is right, and the humble He teaches His way." (Psalm 25:9)

God will teach you if you are humble and teachable. He will show you exactly what to do to center your life around His indwelling presence and to consistently draw closer to Him. "Without having seen Him, you love Him; though you do not [even] now see Him, you believe in Him and exult and thrill with inexpressible and glorious (triumphant, heavenly) joy." (I Peter 1:8)

Even though you have never seen God with your physical eyesight, you can be constantly aware of His indwelling presence. We show our love for God by consistently obeying the specific instructions He has given to us in the holy Scriptures (see John 4:24 and I John 2:5 and 5:3).

Make the decision to renew your mind each day by studying the Word of God (see II Corinthians 4:16 and Ephesians 4:22-23) and meditating day and night on the holy Scriptures (see Joshua 1:8 and Psalm 1:1-3). Show your love for God by consistently learning and obeying the instructions He has given to you in His Word.

In this chapter we have begun to study Scripture about developing a closer and more intimate relationship with God. In the next chapter we will expand this teaching so that you will learn more from God's Word about how to consistently draw closer to God, to center your life continually around His indwelling presence and to know that you are never alone.

Chapter 11

You Will Never Be Lonely

Once you understand the vital importance of focusing your life around the indwelling presence of the Lord, you might be motivated to make a commitment to pay the necessary price to know God better. "...pursue that consecration and holiness without which no one will [ever] see the Lord." (Hebrews 12:14)

The word "consecration" means to devote yourself entirely to reverence for God. Holiness is focusing completely upon exalting God. If you make the commitment to revere God and exalt Him and center your life around Him, you will know Him more intimately. "...consider yourselves also dead to sin and your relation to it broken, but alive to God [living in unbroken fellowship with Him] in Christ Jesus." (Romans 6:11)

Turn away from any sinful habits that are caused by putting yourself first ahead of God. Put God in first place where He belongs. Keep Him there. The amplification in this verse instructs you to live in "unbroken fellowship" with God. The word "unbroken" means constant. Continually draw closer to God. Center your life around Him. "The secret [of the sweet, satisfying companionship] of the Lord have they who fear (revere and worship) Him..." (Psalm 25:14)

This verse tells you the secret of enjoying a close and intimate relationship with God. When you fear God, you revere Him. You worship Him. You hold Him in absolute awe. Every aspect of your life revolves around Him. "...Fear God [revere and worship Him, knowing that He is] and keep His commandments, for this is the whole of man [the full, original purpose of his creation, the object of God's providence, the root of character, the foundation of all happiness, the adjustment to all inharmonious circumstances and conditions under the sun] and the whole [duty] for every man." (Ecclesiastes 12:13)

Please note the words "the full, original purpose of his creation" in the second amplification in this verse. God created you to fear Him and to revere Him. You are told in this amplification that fearing God and obeying His instructions are "the root of character and the foundation of all happiness." Surrendered Christians fear God. Surrendered Christians live happy, meaningful and fulfilling lives.

Are you in awe every time you think that the Creator of all of the billions of people who have ever lived and of everything in the entire universe lives in *your* heart? Do you fully grasp the magnificence of this great spiritual truth? If you do, you will have a commitment that is similar to the apostle Paul's commitment to continually draw closer to Jesus Christ. Paul said, "...I count everything as loss compared to the possession of the priceless privilege (the overwhelming preciousness, the surpassing worth, and supreme advantage) of knowing Christ Jesus my Lord and of progressively becoming more deeply and intimately acquainted with Him [of perceiving and recognizing and understanding Him more fully and clearly]. For His sake I have lost everything and consider it all to be mere rubbish (refuse, dregs), in order that I may win (gain) Christ (the Anointed One)." (Philippians 3:8)

Paul spoke of "the priceless privilege" of knowing Jesus Christ more intimately. What could possibly be more important than to continually draw closer to Jesus Christ Who lives in your heart?

Paul said that everything else was "mere rubbish" in comparison to his deep commitment to know Christ more intimately. Shortly after the verse of Scripture that we just read Paul went on to say, "[For my determined purpose is] that I may know Him [that I may progressively become more deeply and intimately acquainted with Him, perceiving and recognizing and understanding the wonders of His Person more strongly and more clearly]..." (Philippians 3:10)

The first two amplifications in this verse explain that Paul was *determined* to "progressively become more deeply and intimately acquainted" with Jesus Christ. When you do something progressively, you are constantly moving closer to whatever goal you are pursuing. Do not allow anything to come ahead of your continual commitment to progressively become more intimately acquainted with the Lord Jesus Christ.

The Word of God tells you exactly what to do to develop a deep and intimate relationship with God Who lives in your heart. "...this is how we may discern [daily, by experience] that we are coming to know Him [to perceive, recognize, understand, and become better acquainted with Him]: if we keep (bear in mind, observe, practice) His teachings (precepts, commandments)." (I John 2:3)

This verse and the amplification explain that you will know God more intimately if you consistently learn and obey the specific instructions that He has given you in His Book of Instructions, the holy Bible. One of these instructions is to love God. Jesus Christ said, "...You shall love the Lord your God with all your heart and with all your soul and with all your mind (intellect). This is the great (most important, principal) and first commandment." (Matthew 22:37-38)

Nothing is more important than to love God "with all your heart and with all your mind." Do you know exactly what the Bible instructs you to do to show God that you love Him? "...the [true] love of God is this: that we do His commands [keep His ordinances and are mindful of His precepts and teaching]. And these orders of His are not irksome (burdensome, oppressive, or grievous)." (I John 5:3)

You show your love for God in direct proportion to the commitment that you make to learn how He instructs you to live and to obey His specific instructions. This verse and the amplification explain that God's instructions are "not irksome, burdensome, oppressive, or grievous." "...he who keeps (treasures) His Word [who bears in mind His precepts, who observes His message in its entirety], truly in him has the love of and for God been perfected (completed, reached maturity). By this we may perceive (know, recognize, and be sure) that we are in Him." (I John 2:5)

The first amplification in this verse instructs you to treat God's Word as the awesome spiritual treasure that it is. If you understand what a great treasure the Bible is, you will be highly motivated to continually learn and obey more and more of God's instructions.

The second amplification instructs you to obey God's Word "in its entirety." Make the commitment to continually learn and obey the specific instructions that your Father has given to you.

If you consistently study and obey God's instructions, your love for God will be perfected. You will be certain that you are in God and that He is in you.

Think of the most intimate relationship that you have with any person on earth. How does this relationship compare to the intimacy of your relationship with God? Do you truly love God more than you love any human being? The more that you love God, the more love you will have for members of your family and other people.

If you had a very close and intimate relationship with your human father, you would never be lonely when you are with him. If you understand that your loving heavenly Father lives in your heart and your life revolves around His indwelling presence and your desire to consistently draw closer to Him, *you will never be lonely*.

People who are lonely look to external sources for companionship. We have studied several verses of

Scripture explaining that your loving Father lives in your heart if Jesus Christ is your Savior. The closer you are to Him, the less lonely you will be.

Mature Christians crave solitude. They yearn to spend quiet time alone with God. They look forward to this daily quiet time. They are *never* lonely because their lives revolve around the intimacy of their relationship with God Who lives in their hearts.

Chapter 12

Trust God Completely

Do you have absolute faith in the reliability of each of the scriptural statements that we have shared with you in this book? God *always* does what He says He will do. "God is faithful (reliable, trustworthy, and therefore ever true to His promise, and He can be depended on)..." (I Corinthians 1:9)

Every one of the promises that we have studied is true. Everything that the Bible says about God, Jesus Christ and the Holy Spirit living in the heart of every Christian is accurate. "...it is impossible for God ever to prove false or deceive us..." (Hebrews 6:18)

If God says that He lives in your heart, you can be absolutely certain that the Creator of the universe does live in your heart if Jesus Christ is your Savior. "...not one thing has failed of all the good things which the Lord your God promised concerning you...." (Joshua 23:14)

This verse says that "not one" of God's promises has failed. God always emphasizes through repetition. You have just read three verses of Scripture assuring you that the Word of God is true. "...whoever leans on, trusts in, and puts his confidence in the Lord is safe and set on high." (Proverbs 29:25)

The word "whoever" in this verse includes *you*. Your Father wants you to lean on Him and to place all of your trust and confidence in Him. He wants you to be absolutely certain that He lives in your heart, that He is with you at all times and that He will keep you safe.

God can see a way out of every problem. Problems that seem to you to have no solution are not difficult for God to solve. Your Father wants you to be *certain* that He *will* bring you safely through every problem you face in direct proportion to your faith in Him. He loves you so much that He said, "...though the mountains should depart and the hills be shaken or removed, yet My love and kindness shall not depart from you..." (Isaiah 54:10)

Your Father loves you with an incredible love that is beyond the limitations of human logic and understanding. Center your life around His indwelling presence. Trust your loving Father to bring you safely through every problem you face. No matter how difficult any problem in your life may be, your Father is right there with you. Refuse to be upset. God said, "...be still, and know (recognize and understand) that I am God...." (Psalm 46:10)

Your Father instructs you to "be still" in the face of adversity. He wants you to trust Him completely because you know that He is God and that He can solve every problem. "...be calm and cool and steady, accept and suffer unflinchingly every hardship..." (II Timothy 4:5)

God instructs you to "be calm and cool and steady" whenever you face adversity. Please note the words "every hardship" in this verse. These words include every problem that you will face in your life. God instructs you to be "unflinching." When people flinch, they draw back. Refuse to allow any problem you face to overwhelm you. "...whoever leans on, trusts in, and is confident in the Lord—happy, blessed, and fortunate is he." (Proverbs 16:20)

The words "whoever" in this verse include you. God promises to bless you if you trust Him completely. "...we take comfort and are encouraged and confidently and boldly say, The Lord is my Helper; I will not be seized with alarm [I will not fear or dread or be terrified]. What can man do to me?" (Hebrews 13:6)

In Chapter 6 we studied Joshua 1:9, Psalm 46:1-2 and Isaiah 41:10. Each of these verses of Scripture instructs you not to be afraid because of your certainty that God is with you. Do not be "seized with alarm." Have absolute faith that the same God Who created you lives in your heart. Be like the apostle Paul who said, "...I have learned how to be content (satisfied to the point where I am not disturbed or disquieted) in whatever state I am." (Philippians 4:11)

Paul said that he had "learned" not to be disturbed regardless of the severity of any problem he faced. Follow Paul's example. Study and meditate daily on the Scripture references in this book and other promises you find in the Bible that pertain to your situation. Trust God totally, completely and absolutely to bring you safely through every problem you face.

Chapter 13

You Can Hear the Voice of God

So far in this book we have studied Scripture that assures you that God lives in the heart of every person who has received Jesus Christ as his or her Savior. In this chapter we will study Scripture that explains how you can hear God speaking to you.

If Jesus Christ is your Savior, you have been given the ability to hear God speaking to you. Jesus said, "Whoever is of God listens to God. [Those who belong to God hear the words of God.]..." (John 8:47)

You belong to God if Jesus Christ is your Savior. He is your Father. You are His beloved child. You have been given the ability to hear Him speaking to you. Do not miss out on the precious privilege of hearing God speaking to you from within your heart throughout every day of your life. Jesus said, "He who has ears to hear, let him be listening and let him consider and perceive and comprehend by hearing." (Matthew 11:15)

Unbelievers cannot hear God's voice. If you are saved, you are given "ears to hear" God speaking to you.

You can "perceive and comprehend" exactly what God wants you to do.

God always emphasizes through repetition. We seldom see the exact same words used in two passages of Scripture. Shortly after speaking the words that we just read in Matthew 11:15, Jesus used the same words to emphasize that God wants you to listen to Him. Jesus said, "He who has ears [to hear], let him be listening and let him consider and perceive and comprehend by hearing." (Matthew 13:9)

There is no question that your Father wants you to listen to His voice. Be like the psalmist who said, "I will listen [with expectancy] to what God the Lord will say..." (Psalm 85:8)

Please note the words "with expectancy" in the amplification of this verse. *Expect* to hear God speaking to you. His Word says that He will speak to you. Believe that your Father always does exactly what He says He will do.

God wants you to listen to Him just as He wanted the Israelites to listen to Him when He spoke these words. Are you *certain* that the same God Who created everything in the entire universe lives in your heart? Do you *expect* Him to speak to you every day of your life? Do you have the same commitment to hear God that Job did when he said, "...I have esteemed and treasured the words of His mouth more than my necessary food." (Job 23:12)

We know that we will starve if we go indefinitely without eating. Hearing God's voice is more important to you in the spiritual realm than feeding your body is in the natural realm. *Treasure* the words that God speaks to you. "...blessings shall come upon you and overtake you if you heed the voice of the Lord your God." (Deuteronomy 28:2)

Your Father will bless you abundantly if you learn how to hear His voice and then do what He instructs you to do. What could be more important than having the Creator of the universe speaking to you every day your life, telling you exactly what He wants you to do? God will give you instructions when you face severe adversity. "He delivers the afflicted in their affliction and opens their ears [to His voice] in adversity." (Job 36:15)

God promises to "open your ears" to His voice when you face adversity. Know that your loving Father will deliver you and bring you through this adversity if you learn to hear what He is saying and you do what He instructs you to do.

What does God's voice sound like? Because God is Almighty and supernaturally powerful, you might expect His voice to be very powerful. "The voice of the Lord is powerful; the voice of the Lord is full of majesty." (Psalm 29:4)

There are times when God's voice is powerful. However, we have learned through experience that God usually speaks to us in "...a still, small voice." (I Kings 19:12)

Even though God is mighty and powerful and His voice can be mighty and powerful, we can tell you from many years of experience that He usually speaks to His children quietly and gently. You will only hear the still, small voice of God speaking to you from deep down within yourself to the degree that you expect to hear

Him speaking to you. God tells you exactly what *not* to do if you want to hear His voice. "...Today, if you will hear His voice, do not harden your hearts..." (Hebrews 3:7-8)

People with hard hearts are proud. Their lives revolve around themselves. Only Christians who are humble and teachable hear God speaking to them. Jesus Christ said, "...Everyone who is of the Truth [who is a friend of the Truth, who belongs to the Truth] hears and listens to My voice." (John 18:37)

How can you hear the voice of Jesus Christ? You will hear His voice if you are "of the Truth, a friend of the Truth and belong to the Truth." What is Jesus referring to when He speaks of Truth? On another occasion He said, "...Your Word is Truth." (John 17:17)

The Word of God is Truth. You will hear God's voice to the degree that your mind and your heart are filled with the Word of God as a result of consistent Bible study and Scripture meditation. Your Father instructs you to renew your mind by studying His Word each day (see II Corinthians 4:16 and Ephesians 4:22-23). He instructs to meditate day and night on His Word (see Psalm 1:1-3 and Joshua 1:8). On another occasion Jesus said, "...If you abide in My word [hold fast to My teachings and live in accordance with them], you are truly My disciples. And you will know the Truth, and the Truth will set you free." (John 8:31-32)

The more that you know the Truth of God's Word, the more you will be set free from adversity because you will be tuned in to hear God speaking to you. God's voice can be compared to a supernatural radio station. You tune in to a radio station by selecting a specific frequency on a radio dial. You tune in to hear your Father speaking to you to the degree that you pay the price of filling your mind with His Word each day as a result of daily Bible study and to the degree that you fill your heart with His Word as a result of meditating day and night on the holy Scriptures.

Sometimes Jesus arose early in the morning to speak with His Father (see Mark 1:35). Sometimes Jesus went away from the crowds to a quiet place to listen to His Father (see Luke 5:16). Spend precious quiet time alone with God each day. The following words that King Solomon spoke to his son are your Father's words to you today. "Blessed [happy, prosperous, to be admired] is the man who listens to me, watching daily at my gates, waiting at my doorposts." (Proverbs 8:34)

Your Father promises to bless you if you listen to Him "daily." He wants your precious quiet time with Him each day to be the foundation of your life. Spend precious time with God each day when you study and meditate on His Word. Pray to Him and worship Him. If you can learn how to hear His voice during your daily quiet time with Him, you then will be able to hear Him speaking to you throughout every day.

Do not wonder if God really does speak to you. *Know* that He speaks to you. Live each day with simple childlike faith that your Father does live in your heart and that He speaks to you continually.

In this chapter we have studied Scripture that assures you that God does speak to His children. In the next two chapters we will study several Scripture references that explain how God will guide you and teach you throughout every day of your life.

Chapter 14

God Will Teach You

If Jesus Christ is your Savior, you are God's child. God is your loving Father. He knows many things that you need to know. He wants to teach you continually.

Jesus Christ is our example in every area. Throughout His earthly ministry Jesus depended on being taught by His Father. Jesus said, "I am able to do nothing from Myself [independently, of My own accord—but only as I am taught by God and as I get His orders]. Even as I hear, I judge [I decide as I am bidden to decide. As the voice comes to Me, so I give a decision], and My judgment is right (just, righteous), because I do not seek or consult My own will [I have no desire to do what is pleasing to Myself, My own aim, My own purpose] but only the will and pleasure of the Father Who sent Me." (John 5:30)

Jesus spoke these words from His humanity as the Son of man. He set down His heavenly power by His own choice when He came from heaven to earth. He said to His Father, "I am able to do nothing from Myself." Jesus knew that He needed to be taught by His Father. He did not want to do what was pleasing to

Him. He wanted to carry out the will of God in every area of His life on earth.

God will teach you just as He taught Jesus when He was on earth. Jesus was able to do what His Father instructed Him to do because He could hear His Father speaking to Him. If you are able to hear God's voice, your loving Father will teach you just as He taught Jesus.

Jesus explained that no one can receive Him as his or her Savior unless God Himself draws that person to Him. Jesus said, "No one is able to come to Me unless the Father Who sent Me attracts and draws him and gives him the desire to come to Me..." (John 6:44)

In the next verse Jesus went on to explain that people who are children of God will be taught by God. Jesus said, "...they shall all be taught of God [have Him in person for their Teacher]. Everyone who has listened to and learned from the Father comes to Me." (John 6:45)

God wants to teach every one of His children. Learn continually from your Father Who lives in your heart. Be like the prophet Isaiah who was certain that God would teach him. Isaiah said, "...He wakens Me morning by morning, He wakens My ear to hear as a disciple [as one who is taught]." (Isaiah 50:4)

God is there for you from the time you wake up in the morning throughout every day of your life. He wants you to constantly be tuned in to His voice so that you can learn from Him.

Only humble Christians can be taught by God. Proud and self-centered people are not teachable because their lives revolve around themselves. If you are in absolute awe because you are certain that your Father lives in your heart and you know that He wants to teach you, you will humble yourself before Him continually. You will yearn to receive supernatural teaching from Him. The psalmist David said, "Show me Your ways, O Lord; teach me Your paths. Guide me in Your truth and faithfulness and teach me, for You are the God of my salvation; for You [You only and altogether] do I wait [expectantly] all the day long." (Psalm 25:4-5)

David constantly turned to God asking Him to teach him and to guide him. He waited expectantly to be taught by God. Follow David's example in your life.

Your Father wants you to be humble and teachable. He wants you to know how much you need to be taught by Him. "...knowledge is easy to him who [being teachable] understands." (Proverbs 14:6)

Your Father will always give you whatever specific knowledge you need when you are teachable. Are you in awe that God lives in your heart? Are you in awe that God wants to teach *you*? Do not reject the tremendous opportunity you have been given to be taught by God Himself. Come to God humbly each day with a yearning to learn from Him continually.

Your Father is very pleased with His children who are humble and teachable (see Luke 14:11, Philippians 2:3-5 and James 4:6). Many of God's children are unaware of the Scripture references that we are studying in this chapter. They do not know that God wants to teach them continually.

A very special secret pertaining to God's principles is to always honor others above yourself (see Luke 14:11). Do your best to honor everyone, rich or poor, educated or uneducated, and those who are similar to you and those who are not (see Philippians 2:3-4).

Another of God's secrets is that, the less you promote yourself, the more He will promote you. As you yield to God, the Holy Spirit will flow freely in your life. You will become someone you never imagined you could be (see James 4:6).

God will teach you if you faithfully obey His instructions to renew your mind by studying His Word *each day* (see II Corinthians 4:16 and Ephesians 4:22-23) and to meditate *day and night* on the holy Scriptures (see Joshua 1:8 and Psalm 1:2-3). The psalmist said, "My lips shall pour forth praise [with thanksgiving and renewed trust] when You teach me Your statutes." (Psalm 119:171)

The psalmist praised God and thanked Him for teaching him from His Word. Your Father wants you to have this same attitude of gratitude. The Bible is His supernatural Book of Instructions. He will teach you from His Book of Instructions. God said, "I [the Lord] will instruct you and teach you in the way you should go; I will counsel you with My eye upon you." (Psalm 32:8)

Please note the words "I will counsel you with My eye upon you" in this verse. God is watching you every day. How very special you are! The prophet Isaiah said, "...your Teacher will not hide Himself any more, but your eyes will constantly behold your Teacher. And your ears will hear a word behind you, saying, This is the way; walk in it, when you turn to the right hand and when you turn to the left." (Isaiah 30:20-21)

Your Teacher lives in your heart. He will tell you when to turn to the right and when to turn to the left. He will teach you every minute detail that you need to know.

When this verse speaks of hearing a voice behind you, the word "behind" refers to the Old Testament primarily emphasizing that God is with you at all times while the New Testament emphasizes that God is in you. If Jesus Christ is your Savior, your Teacher lives in your heart.

Jesus Christ taught His disciples throughout His earthly ministry. When He told His disciples that He would be ascending to heaven, He assured them that God would send the Holy Spirit to teach them continually just as He had taught them. Jesus said, "...the Comforter (Counselor, Helper, Intercessor, Advocate, Strengthener, Standby), the Holy Spirit, Whom the Father will send in My name [in My place, to represent Me and act on My behalf], He will teach you all things..." (John 14:26)

In Chapter 2 we studied Scripture about God living in your heart. In Chapter 3 we studied Scripture about Jesus Christ living in your heart. In Chapter 4 we studied Scripture about the Holy Spirit living in your heart.

If Jesus Christ is your Savior, the Holy Spirit is your Teacher. He yearns to teach you continually. Please note the words "He will teach you all things" in this verse. There is no limit to what the Holy Spirit will teach you except any limit that you set by not expecting Him to teach you whatever you need to know.

Chapter 15

God Will Guide You Continually

In the last chapter we studied several Scripture references pertaining to being taught by God. In this chapter we will study Scripture explaining that, in addition to teaching you, God will guide you throughout your life if you can hear His voice. "...God is our God forever and ever; He will be our guide [even] until death." (Psalm 48:14)

Your Father promises to guide you throughout your life up until the time you die. You have a supernatural lifetime guide living in your heart. He will tell you exactly what He wants you to do. He will explain how to do what He wants you to do. "...the Lord shall guide you continually..." (Isaiah 58:11)

God promises to guide you continually. Not one hour of your life goes by where God is not right there with you waiting to guide you. Your Father will guide you if you trust Him instead of trusting yourself. "...cease from your own [human] wisdom." (Proverbs 23:4)

Your Father wants you to turn away from the limitations of your human understanding. "Lean on, trust in, and be confident in the Lord with all your heart and mind and do not rely on your own insight or understanding. In all your ways know, recognize, and acknowledge Him, and He will direct and make straight and plain your paths." (Proverbs 3:5-6)

Many people are concerned when they face severe adversity because they think that they have to solve difficult problems with their limited human abilities. God's Word says, "Do *not* rely on your own insight or understanding." Place all of your trust and confidence in God to guide you and to direct you continually. "...the Lord will grant you full insight and understanding in everything." (II Timothy 2:7)

Please note the word "everything" in this verse. Your Father promises to give you "full insight and understanding" at all times. "If any of you is deficient in wisdom, let him ask of the giving God [Who gives] to everyone liberally and ungrudgingly, without reproaching or faultfinding, and it will be given him." (James 1:5)

Are you "deficient in wisdom"? Ask God to give you His wisdom. He promises to give supernatural wisdom to you "liberally." "Happy (blessed, fortunate, enviable) is the man who finds skillful and godly Wisdom, and the man who gets understanding [drawing it forth from God's Word and life's experiences], for the gaining of it is better than the gaining of silver, and the profit of it better than fine gold." (Proverbs 3:13-14)

You will be happy and blessed if you learn how to receive wisdom from God. Your loving Father will give you full understanding if you obey His instructions to renew your mind by studying His Word each day (see

Colossians 4:16 and Ephesians 4:22-23) and if you obey His instructions to meditate day and night on the holy Scriptures (see Joshua 1:8 and Psalm 1:1-3).

Receiving wisdom, guidance and understanding from God is more profitable to you than any amount of money in the world. The following words that King Solomon spoke to his son are God's words to you today. "Get skillful and godly Wisdom, get understanding (discernment, comprehension, and interpretation); do not forget and do not turn back from the words of my mouth. Forsake not [Wisdom], and she will keep, defend, and protect you; love her, and she will guard you." (Proverbs 4:5-6)

Your Father wants you to be fully aware of His repeated assurances that He *will* give you wisdom and understanding and that He *will* guide you. God said, "...I will bring the blind by a way that they know not; I will lead them in paths that they have not known. I will make darkness into light before them and make uneven places into a plain. These things I have determined to do [for them]; and I will not leave them forsaken." (Isaiah 42:16)

When you cannot see any way out of a difficult problem, God can see the way out. He will show you ways that you "know not." He will tell you everything that you need to know. He will never forsake you. "A man's mind plans his way, but the Lord directs his steps and makes them sure." (Proverbs 16:9)

Human beings plan what they want to do. Do not limit yourself to human planning. God promises to "direct your steps and make them sure." "The steps of a [good] man are directed and established by the Lord when He delights in his way [and He busies Himself with his every step]." (Psalm 37:23)

When this verse and the amplification refer to "a good man," these words refer to any man or woman who is righteous before God as a result of receiving Jesus Christ as his or her Savior. You are a child of God if Jesus Christ is your Savior. Your loving Father will direct you if you turn to Him with absolute trust. He "delights" in helping you every step of the way throughout your life.

Not only will your Father guide you in whatever you do, but He also will guide you in the words that you speak. We see an excellent example of God speaking through human beings in the life of Moses. Moses was a great man of God, but he knew that he was not eloquent. "...Moses said to the Lord, O Lord, I am not eloquent or a man of words, neither before nor since You have spoken to Your servant; for I am slow of speech and have a heavy and awkward tongue." (Exodus 4:10)

God encouraged Moses. He told Moses that he would not have to depend on his human ability to speak words. God said, "...go, and I will be with your mouth and will teach you what you shall say." (Exodus 4:12)

You have learned that God is with you at all times. Open your mouth with absolute faith that God will speak through you. Jesus Christ said, "...do not be anxious about how or what you are to speak; for what you are to say will be given you in that very hour and moment, for it is not you who are speaking, but the Spirit of your Father speaking through you." (Matthew 10:19-20)

These words that Jesus spoke to His disciples many years ago are His words to you today. When you face a difficult problem and you do not know what to say, do not worry. The Holy Spirit Who lives in your heart will speak through you in direct proportion to your faith in Him. Jesus said, "...when He, the Spirit of Truth (the Truth-giving Spirit) comes, He will guide you into all the Truth (the whole, full Truth). For He will not speak His own message [on His own authority]; but He will tell whatever He hears [from the Father; He will give the message that has been given to Him], and He will announce and declare to you the things that are to come [that will happen in the future]." (John 16:13)

Once again these words that Jesus spoke to His disciples also are His words to you today. If Jesus Christ is your Savior, the Holy Spirit lives in your heart. He will guide you continually. The Holy Spirit hears directly from God. He will tell you what God says to Him. He also will give you knowledge of what will happen in the future.

This chapter is filled with Scripture references pertaining to receiving wisdom and guidance from God. Your Father lives in your heart. He will never forsake you. He will guide you throughout your life if your life revolves around His indwelling presence and if you trust Him to teach you, help you and guide you throughout your life.

Conclusion

This book is filled with God's instructions pertaining to His indwelling presence. God lives in your heart. Jesus Christ lives in your heart. The Holy Spirit lives in your heart. If Jesus Christ is your Savior, you have inside of you everything that you will ever need.

Please pray about sharing a copy of this book with your friends and loved ones. This book is filled with Scripture references pertaining to God's indwelling presence. Be sure that your friends and loved ones know that God comes to live in the heart of every Christian. Help these people to learn what you have learned in regard to the power that your Father has promised to every person who consistently centers his or her life around His indwelling presence.

In order to enable you to purchase several copies of our publications, we provide a 40% discount for 5-9 items and a 50% discount for any 10 or more items. From our beginning God has instructed us to give our readers similar discounts to the discounts that bookstores receive when they purchase books in quantity. See the order form at the back of this book or online at www.lamplight.net.

If this book has helped you, would you share your testimony with us so that we can share with others what

God has done in your life through *God Lives in the Heart of Every Christian*? We normally need three to four paragraphs in a testimony so that we can consolidate this information into one solid paragraph for our newsletter and our website. Your comments will encourage many people, including pastors and leaders in Third World countries and inmates in prisons and jails who receive our books free of charge. We have received comments from *people in 61 countries* who have been helped by our books, Scripture cards and CDs.

Please send any comments that you have to us at lamplightmin@yahoo.com. You can call 1-800-540-1597 and leave a message for Judy. You also can mail your comments to Lamplight Ministries, Inc., PO Box 1307, Dunedin, FL 34697.

We invite you to visit our website: www.lamplight.net. You will find many comments from people who have been helped by our books, Scripture cards and CDs. You also will find a section on biblical health as well as recipes that Judy adds each month to bless you. We are in good health at ages 84 and 76. I know that I would not be alive today if it were not for Judy's knowledge and wisdom regarding health and her amazing recipes. Judy has a monthly bulletin "Biblical Health in a Nutshell" on our website.

You can keep in touch with us on Facebook (facebook.com/jackandjudylamplight) and Twitter (twitter.com/lamplightmin). You can follow our blog at lamplightmin.wordpress.com You can receive frequent updates on our latest books. You can order our books as e-books at SmashWords.com – enter "Jack Hartman."

We ask you to pray for us. Even though we are at an age where most people are completely retired, we are completing two books each year with no foreseeable plans to stop delivering God's Word to readers with a simple and easy-to-understand explanation. Your prayers for us will make a difference.

We have been blessed to share with you the results of hundreds of hours that we have invested to explain what the Word of God teaches about the indwelling presence of God. We are waiting to hear about your journey with Jesus Christ through this book. We are looking forward to hearing from you.

Blessed to be a blessing. (Genesis 12:1-3)

Jack and Judy

Appendix

Trust Jesus Christ as Your Savior

This book is filled with instructions and promises from God. However, if you have not received Jesus Christ as your Savior, you cannot understand the scriptural truths that are contained in this book. "...the mind of the flesh [with its carnal thoughts and purposes] is hostile to God, for it does not submit itself to God's Law; indeed it cannot." (Romans 8:7)

Please notice the word "cannot" in this verse of Scripture. If Jesus Christ is not your Savior, you cannot possibly understand and obey God's instructions.

Many people who have not received Christ as their Savior are not open to the specific instructions that God has given to us in the Bible. "...the natural, nonspiritual man does not accept or welcome or admit into his heart the gifts and teachings and revelations of the Spirit of God, for they are folly (meaningless nonsense) to him; and he is incapable of knowing them [of progressively recognizing, understanding, and becoming better acquainted with them] because they are spiritually discerned and estimated and appreciated." (I Corinthians 2:14)

The words "does not accept or welcome or admit into his heart the gifts and teachings and revelations of the Spirit of God" in this verse are very important. Some people are opposed to the Bible and what it teaches. They look at Scripture references as "meaningless nonsense." These people are "incapable of" learning great scriptural truths from God until and unless they receive Jesus Christ as their Savior.

At the close of this Appendix we will explain exactly what God instructs you to do to receive Jesus Christ as your Savior. If and when you make this decision, the glorious supernatural truths of the Bible will open up to you. Jesus said, "...To you it has been given to know the secrets and mysteries of the kingdom of heaven, but to them it has not been given." (Matthew 13:11)

Jesus was speaking to *you* when He said that you can "know the secrets and mysteries of the kingdom of heaven." Do not miss out on the glorious privilege that is available to every believer to know and understand the ways of God.

A spiritual veil blocks all unbelievers from understanding the ways of God. "...even if our Gospel (the glad tidings) also be hidden (obscured and covered up with a veil that hinders the knowledge of God), it is hidden [only] to those who are perishing and obscured [only] to those who are spiritually dying and veiled [only] to those who are lost." (II Corinthians 4:3)

This spiritual veil is pulled aside when you receive Jesus Christ as your Savior. "...whenever a person turns [in repentance] to the Lord, the veil is stripped off and taken away." (II Corinthians 3:16)

If you obey the scriptural instructions at the end of this Appendix, Jesus Christ will become your Savior. Everything in your life will become fresh and new. "...if any person is [ingrafted] in Christ (the Messiah) he is a new creation (a new creature altogether); the old [previous moral and spiritual condition] has passed away. Behold, the fresh and new has come!" (II Corinthians 5:17)

Instead of being opposed to the teachings of the holy Bible, you will be completely open to these teachings. You will have a hunger and thirst to continually learn more supernatural truths from the Word of God. "...I endorse and delight in the Law of God in my inmost self [with my new nature]." (Romans 7:22)

Every person who has not received Jesus Christ as his or her Savior is a sinner who is doomed to live throughout eternity in the horror of hell. God has made it possible for *you* to escape this terrible eternal penalty. "...God so greatly loved and dearly prized the world that He [even] gave up His only begotten (unique) Son, so that whoever believes in (trusts in, clings to, relies on) Him shall not perish (come to destruction, be lost) but have eternal (everlasting) life." (John 3:16)

God knew that everyone who lived on earth after Adam and Eve would be a sinner because of the sins of Adam and Eve (see Romans 3:10-12). He sent His only Son from heaven to earth to take upon Himself the sins of the world when He died a horrible death by crucifixion. If you believe that Jesus Christ paid the full price for your sins and if you trust Him completely for your eternal salvation, you will live with Him throughout eternity in the glory of heaven.

There is only *one* way for you to live eternally in heaven after you die – that is to receive eternal salvation through Jesus Christ. "Jesus said to him, I am the Way and the Truth and the Life; no one comes to the Father except by (through) Me." (John 14:6)

If you trust in anyone or anything except Jesus Christ for your eternal salvation, you will not live eternally in heaven. If you are reading these truths about living eternally in heaven because of the price that Jesus Christ has paid for you, you can be certain that the same God Who created you actually is drawing you to come to Jesus Christ for eternal salvation. Jesus said, "No one is able to come to Me unless the Father Who sent Me attracts and draws him and gives him the desire to come to Me..." (John 6:44)

Are you interested in these spiritual truths about where you will live throughout eternity? If you are, you can be certain that the same awesome God Who created you is drawing *you* to Jesus Christ at this very moment.

Heaven is a glorious place. Everyone in heaven is completely healthy and very happy. "God will wipe away every tear from their eyes; and death shall be no more, neither shall there be anguish (sorrow and mourning) nor grief nor pain any more, for the old conditions and the former order of things have passed away." (Revelation 21:4)

All of the problems of earth will disappear when you are in heaven. No one in heaven dies. No one in heaven is sad. No one in heaven cries. No one in heaven suffers from pain.

You *will* live throughout eternity in one place or another. If you do not receive Jesus Christ as your

Savior, you will live eternally in hell. People in hell will experience continual torment throughout eternity. "...the smoke of their torment ascends forever and ever; and they have no respite (no pause, no intermission, no rest, no peace) day or night..." (Revelation 14:11)

Everyone in heaven is filled with joy. Everyone in hell is miserable. Jesus described what hell would be like when He said, "...there will be weeping and wailing and grinding of teeth. (Matthew 13:42)

The inhabitants of hell will weep and wail throughout eternity. They will grind their teeth in anguish. Can you imagine living this way for the endless trillions of years of eternity? This is exactly what will happen if you *reject* the supreme sacrifice that Jesus Christ made to pay the full price for your sins.

How do you receive eternal salvation through Jesus Christ? "...if you acknowledge and confess with your lips that Jesus is Lord and in your heart believe (adhere to, trust in, and rely on the truth) that God raised Him from the dead, you will be saved. For with the heart a person believes (adheres to, trusts in, and relies on Christ) and so is justified (declared righteous, acceptable to God), and with the mouth he confesses (declares openly and speaks out freely his faith) and confirms [his] salvation." (Romans 10:9-10)

Repent of your sins. You must *believe in your heart* (not just think in your mind) that Jesus Christ paid the full price for all of your sins when He was crucified. You must believe that God actually raised Jesus from the dead. You must open your mouth and *speak* this truth that you believe in your heart. If you believe in your heart that Jesus Christ died and rose again from the dead and that the price for your sins has been paid for and you tell others that you believe this great spiritual truth, you have been saved. You *will* live eternally in heaven.

If Jesus Christ was not your Savior when you began to read this book, we pray that He is your Savior now. If He is your Savior, your life will change immensely. You will never be the same again. Every aspect of your life will be gloriously new.

If you have become a child of God by receiving eternal salvation through Jesus Christ, please let us know by contacting us at lamplightmin@yahoo.com, 1-800-540-1497 or PO Box 1307, Dunedin, FL 34697. We would like to pray for you and welcome you as our new Christian brother or sister. We love you and bless you in the name of our Lord Jesus Christ.

We would be so pleased to hear from you. If you are already a believer, we would be pleased to hear from you as well. We invite you to visit our website at www.lamplight.net. Please let us know if this book or one or more of our other publications has made a difference in your life. Please give us your comments so that we can share these comments in our newsletters and on our website to encourage other people.

Study Guide

What Did You Learn From This Book?

The questions in this Study Guide are carefully arranged to show you how much you have learned about God living in your heart. This Study Guide is not intended to be an academic test. The sole purpose of the following questions is to help you increase your practical knowledge pertaining to God living in your heart, Jesus Christ living in your heart, and the Holy Spirit living in your heart.

Page number

1. How can you be certain that God Who sits on His throne in heaven also lives in your heart if Jesus Christ is your Savior? (Ephesians 4:6, Jeremiah 23:24 and I John 4:15) 13-14

2. If Jesus Christ is your Savior, how can you be certain that the same God Who created everything in the universe is your Father and that you are His beloved child? (Galatians 3:26, Romans 8:16, Galatians 4:6, John 1:12-13, Ephesians 2:19, II Corinthians 6:18 and I John 3:1) 14-16

A Few Words About Lamplight Ministries

Lamplight Ministries, Inc. originally began in 1983 as Lamplight Publications. After ten years as a publishing firm with the goal of selling Christian books, Lamplight Ministries was established in 1991. Jack and Judy Hartman founded Lamplight Ministries with a mission of continuing to sell their publications and also to *give* large numbers of these publications free of charge to needy people all over the world.

Lamplight Ministries was created to allow people who have been blessed by our publications to share in financing the translation, printing and distribution of our books into other languages and also to distribute our publications free of charge to inmates in jails and prisons. Over the years many partners of Lamplight Ministries have shared Jack and Judy's vision. Thousands of people in jails and prisons and in Third World countries have received our publications free of charge.

Our books and Scripture Meditation Cards have been translated into eleven foreign languages – Armenian, Danish, Greek, Hebrew, German, Korean, Norwegian, Portuguese, Russian, Spanish and the

Tamil dialect in India. The translations in these languages are not available from Lamplight Ministries in the United States. These translations can only be obtained in the countries where we have given permission for them to be published.

The pastors of many churches in Third World countries have written to say that they consistently preach sermons in their churches based on the scriptural contents of our publications. We believe that people in several churches in many different countries hear sermons that are based on the scriptural contents of our publications. Praise the Lord!

Jack Hartman was the sole author of twelve Christian books. After co-authoring one book with Judy, Jack and Judy co-authored ten sets of Scripture Meditation Cards. Judy has been the co-author of every subsequent book. Jack and Judy currently are working on other books that they believe the Lord is leading them to write as co-authors.

We invite you to request our newsletters to stay in touch with us, to learn of our latest publications and to read comments from people all over the world. Please write, fax, call or email us. You are very special to us. We love you and thank God for you. Our heart is to take the gospel to the world and for our books to be available in every known language. Hallelujah!

Lamplight Ministries, Inc.,
PO Box 1307 - Dunedin, Florida, 34697. USA
Phone: 1-800-540-1597
Fax: 1-727-784-2980
website: lamplight.net
email: lamplightmin@yahoo.com

We offer you a substantial quantity discount

From the beginning of our ministry we have been led of the Lord to offer the same quantity discount to individuals that we offer to Christian bookstores. Each individual has a sphere of influence with a specific group of people. We believe that you know many people who need to learn the scriptural contents of our publications.

The Word of God encourages us to give freely to others. We encourage you to give selected copies of these publications to people you know who need help in the specific areas that are covered by our publications. See our order form for specific information on the quantity discounts that we make available to you so that you can share our books, Scripture Meditation Cards and CDs with others.

A request to our readers

If this book has helped you, we would like to receive your comments so that we can share them with others. Your comments can encourage other people to study our publications to learn from the scriptural contents of these publications.

When we receive a letter containing comments on any of our books, cassette tapes or Scripture Meditation Cards, we prayerfully take out excerpts from these letters. These selected excerpts are included in our newsletters and occasionally in our advertising and promotional materials.

If any of our publications have been a blessing to you, please share your comments with us so that we can share them with others. Tell us in your own words what a specific publication has meant to you and why you would recommend it to others. Please give as much specific information as possible. We prefer three or four paragraphs so that we can condense this into one paragraph.

Thank you for taking a few minutes of your time to encourage other people to learn from the scripture references in our publications.

Enthusiastic Comments from Readers of our Publications

The following are just a few of the many comments we have received from people in *61 countries* pertaining to our publications. For additional comments, see our website: lamplight.net.

Trust God for Your Finances

There are more than 150,000 copies of *Trust God for Your Finances* in print. This book has been translated into seven foreign languages.

- "I have translated *Trust God for Your Finances* into Thai. I intended to make about 50 or 60 photocopies of this translation to distribute among friends. My pastor asked for 700 copies to distribute at the special yearly conference for pastors. My immediate thought was that I could not do this, but he urged me to pray and try my best. Surprisingly, it worked out. Thank God. More than 1,000 people attended the conference. Seven hundred copies were distributed to only the pastors, elders and deacons who really wanted the book. After the conference, we had so many calls that another 2,000 copies were printed. Thank you, Mr. Hartman, for this book

which is helping so many Thai Christians."
(Thailand)

- "I bought your book, *Trust God for Your Finances,*
at a church I was attending in Virginia in the 1980s.
This book transformed my life. It was all Bible-based
and solid in every way. I married a Bulgarian pastor
who started the church here during Communism
and the underground church. We have pastored
together for 22 years. I gave your book to my
husband and he consumed it. He kept it near his
Bible all the time. God has raised him up to be
influential in this nation. He has written a book titled
The Covenant of Provision dealing with finances.
Your book helped him so much to form his ideas
about the rightful use of money. This book has
influenced my husband more than almost any other
book. It was so timely and needed coming out of a
Communist society. Thank you so much for this
book." (Bulgaria)

- "Today we had a ministry partner join us for lunch.
He said that the book, *Trust God for Your Finances,*
that we had translated into Hebrew was the most
powerful book he had ever read on the subject. I
shared with him the wonderful story of how you
shared the book with us and how many Israelis have
been enlightened in that area as a result of reading
the book. You both are a blessing and a treasure in
God's kingdom." (Israel)

The Rapture and the Second Coming of Christ
- "Thank you for offering to send us a free copy of
your new book, *The Rapture and the Second
Coming of Christ.* Please send me a copy of this

book. Your books are easy to read, especially for those people here who do not speak English well. We had a copy of the last book that you sent us in our Church Library. It is now worn out because so many people borrowed it. Could you send us some additional books?" (Ghana)

- "Your book, *The Rapture and the Second Coming of Christ*, is a wonderful book. The Scripture in this book has greatly expanded the limited knowledge that I had pertaining to this subject. I have been teaching from this book for several weeks to our Sunday school class. This book has been an eye-opener to the members of our class. Several people who used to come to the class occasionally now are attending every week. They do not miss a week. We have received an exceptional response to your book. Thank you so much for writing it." (Iowa)

- "Thank you for the simplicity in your beautifully written book *The Rapture and the Second Coming of Christ*. This book was so understandable and complete with Scripture. God bless you in your love for Him and through Him." (Massachusetts)

What Does God Say?
- "Your book *What Does God Say?* is one of the greatest books I have ever read. You tell the truth and back it up with Scripture. I started crime very young. I have spent a large portion of my life behind bars. I have so much to be ashamed of and things that I am very sorry for. I have almost wasted my life. I say almost because this book caused me to realize that God loves even me no matter what I have done. In your book I read that there is no

condemnation in Christ Jesus. Do you have any idea what it means to feel no condemnation when society says to lock me up because I am guilty? My sins and all the crimes I have committed have been washed away. I cannot explain how it feels to know that someone is really proud of me. That someone is Jesus. I am taking this book home with me. Even though I don't have much education, I can understand it very well. I now know that I am saved and I am forgiven. Thank you very much for writing this book." (Florida)

- "Several months ago, you sent me a copy of your book titled *What Does God Say?*. This book is amazing. First of all, I could understand it. My English is not great. I have been a Muslim all my life. I was taught as a child what I was supposed to believe. When I was searching for real truth, I met the Master and received Jesus Christ as my Savior. When I read your book, it filled so much of the void and loneliness that I was filled with. I will be sharing Jesus and *What Does God Say?* with my family and with other Muslims. Please pray for me as I may not be welcomed in my own home town for finding this wonderful Jesus." (Ghana)

- "Our ministry here in South Africa is flourishing. We thank God for the books from Jack and Judy Hartman. The book, *What Does God Say?*, is my daily manual. It addresses all issues of life. I read it every day and I love it. I am complete. This book has made our ministry more effective. I no longer have to struggle on what to preach or teach. I am now equipped with the correct material. This book is filled with the anointing and revelation of God.

My fellow pastors here in South Africa are hungry for these books. We soon will be opening a branch in Pretoria and also in Botswana. I thank God for the Hartmans. I always pray for them." (South Africa)

Quiet Confidence in the Lord

- "As soon as I was diagnosed with prostate cancer, I began to meditate on the Scripture and your explanation of the Scripture in *Quiet Confidence in the Lord*. I carried this book with me everywhere for several weeks. The specialist at the Lahey Clinic in Boston told me I was the calmest person with this diagnosis that he had ever seen. During the pre-op and the surgery, a number of people commented on how calm I was. I experienced a lot of discomfort during the difficult first week at home after the surgery. I focused constantly on the Scripture in this wonderful book. I was remarkably calm. Thank you for writing this book that has helped me so much." (Massachusetts)

- "After I graduated from Bible school, I went outside of my country for mission work with my wife. After we were there for nine months, my wife died suddenly. My sorrow was great. I read your book titled *Quiet Confidence in the Lord*. This book spoke to my heart. All twenty-three chapters were written for me. God changed me through this book and comforted me and took away my sorrow. Through the blood of Jesus I entered God's rest. I can give a great recommendation for this book to anyone who is filled with sorrow and grief. I pray that many people will read this book and develop quiet confidence in the Lord as I did. Thank you so much for sending this book to me. May God bless you and your ministry." (Ethiopia)

- "*Quiet Confidence in the Lord* is with me at work each day. I have read and underlined passages that lift my heart and help me to understand something I've known all along and that is that I am not alone and that God cares very much that I'm in the midst of great adversity. I asked God to send me a comforter, someone who would put their arms around me and say, 'I understand and I care.' The answer to that prayer is in you and Judy. Thanks to *Quiet Confidence of the Lord* I am, for the first time in my life, learning to focus on God and not my problems. Thank you both for your ministry. Your books are a tremendous blessing to hurting people all over the world." (Washington, DC)

God's Instructions for Growing Older
- "I am a 63-year-old businesswoman from Thailand. Like most women around the world, I do not like growing old. When I received a copy of your book, *God's Instructions For Growing Older*, I read straight from the first page to the last in two days. Your book gives me the assurance of how to grow older without fear, anxiety, and worry. I will live the rest of my life in peace and joy for I now know that if we keep God in first place at all times, the final years of our lives will be meaningful, productive, and fulfilling. Thank you, Mr. and Mrs. Hartman, for the priceless gift of your book. May God bless you and your team always." (Thailand)

- "I have never read a book like *God's Instructions for Growing Older*. Finally a book has been written that teaches how to finish our course in life as a Christian. Your chapter on Scripture meditation is pure gold. This book is a road map to direct us in the way the Lord intends for us to grow older. Thank you so much for this special book." (Florida)
- "Thank you for your new book, *God's Instructions for Growing Older*. I love this book. I read a little bit every day so that I can be an encourager to my older friends and to myself. We so need God's knowledge during the final years of our lives. I have started my gift list to share this book with others." (Texas)

Receive Healing from the Lord
- "Your great book, *Receive Healing from the Lord*, has amazed me. This book has been my daily bread. I have followed all of God's instructions in your book. My children and my wife were healed from severe illness. I was sick myself just before an important crusade. I meditated on the Scripture in your book for the entire night. I was totally healed. The following day God did wonders as He healed many people. Since then, people have been coming to receive their healing at our home and church almost every day. Many healings are taking place at our services. This book is wonderful. I am abundantly blessed by it." (Zambia)
- "My husband and I served in the mission field in Swaziland, Africa, for three and a half years. Upon our arrival, Lamplight Ministries sent us four mailbags full of Jack and Judy's books. Because

Swaziland is so laden with HIV/AIDS, we were able to use the book, *Receive Healing from the Lord,* with the people in Swaziland to see many people come to a saving knowledge of the Lord Jesus Christ and His perfect will regarding healing. We saw mothers with very sick children who themselves also were afflicted with AIDS respond to the many Scriptures that are part of the book, actually believing that it was meant for them. Had it not been for the use of this book and the other books you sent, we would not have had such success in teaching a Bible study about the truth in God's Word to these people. We gave out your books and told the people that the book was theirs to keep. We saw such joy and surprise on the faces of these impoverished people. We appreciate the ongoing generosity of Lamplight Ministries for 'such a time as this' in these days where there is so much need and want. We will forever be thankful that we can count on the Word of God through the books written by Jack and Judy as effective tools in the transformation of people's lives." (Swaziland)

- "Thank you very much for sending me your book, *Receive Healing from the Lord.* After reading the first chapter I realized that this book could be the solution for my wife's failing health. We decided to read the book together every day. My wife was healed and restored after carefully following the scriptural principles that you explained. We are humbled by how we had struggled and panicked trying to find an answer. God gave us the solution in your book. We are so grateful to you. We love you and we are praying for you." (Zambia)

You Can Hear the Voice of God

- "Many years of my life I scoffed at Christians. I looked at them as holy rollers. When I was incarcerated, I experienced pain as I have never felt in my life. A darkness and loneliness like I have never experienced before came upon me. A friend here gave me your book, *You Can Hear the Voice of God*. If there ever was a time when I needed to hear from God, it is now. My wife was desperately ill at the very point of death when I started reading your book. I now know that God has been trying to talk to me all of my life, but I didn't know how to listen to His voice. NOW I CAN HEAR THE VOICE OF GOD. In a splendid and simple way you actually taught me how to hear the voice of God Almighty. How can I ever thank you? Thank you for writing this book. It will impact hundreds of thousands, I am sure." (Florida)

- "Thank you for sending me a copy of *You Can Hear the Voice of God*. This book is so good. On the first day of having this book in my hands, I read continually. I finished five chapters. My wife was invited to teach at a meeting of pastors' wives. The women were excited because of this teaching. I would like to translate this book into Benba, one of the largest spoken languages on the copper belt and some provinces of Zambia. Would you give me permission to translate this book? I know that the Holy Spirit has inspired me to do so." (Zambia) (Permission was granted.)

- "Thank you for the box of books that you sent to a pastor who is a friend of mine. He gave me a copy of your book *You Can Hear The Voice of God*. This book is a spiritual manual for the serious Christian. I thank God for Jack and Judy Hartman. This book is helping me to draw closer to my Maker. I now realize that God has been talking to me daily but I did not hear Him. This book is a real blessing to the body of Christ." (Ghana)

God's Plan for Your Life

- "Your book, *God's Plan for Your Life,* has been a blessing in my life. You emphasize turning away from the pursuit of empty worldly goals to devote our lives to doing what God has called us to do. These are wise words. I agree with you wholeheartedly and I am following your advice. I felt very satisfied and fulfilled after reading this book. Thank you, Mr. and Mrs. Hartman, for being such dedicated servants of the Lord." (Thailand)

- "My wife and I enjoy your books. We always draw inspiration from your writing. *God's Plan for Your Life* is a great resource. This book has stimulated our lives. We have discovered many things we did not know before. We are teaching in our church from this book. Knowing that the Lord has good plans for us gives us the fuel to face each day with zeal and courage. God bless you and keep you." (Zambia)

- "Thank you so much for the inspiration and hope that breathes through your precious book, *God's Plan for Your Life.* This book has helped me during the dark hours of my life when everything seemed lost and there did not seem to be any way out. I have known God most of my life, but I got ahead of Him. I know now that God has everything under control when I seek Him." (Florida)

- "Thank you for sending me your book, *God's Plan for Your Life*, free of charge. After reading this book I am totally convinced that you have God Almighty's anointing to write for Him. The first chapter is a revelation. After I read this chapter I had a strong urge to continue reading. I could not put the book down. God is great! I am finding the book to be the answer to many of our three teenage sons' questions. I have noticed that my 15-year-old son is the main beneficiary. He now prays and fasts more and is doing other things that he never did before. He also is asking God to reveal His plan for his life." (Zimbabwe)

Glorious Eternal Life in Heaven
- "Greetings in Jesus' mighty name. I am excited to report that *Glorious Eternal Life in Heaven* is one of the best books I have ever read. This book will be a major resource for me as I prepare to teach others that we are free from the bondage of death. God bless you and give you long life to continue to sow the precious seeds of the Word of Life to many people. Be blessed, for great is your reward." (Kenya)
- "Dear Papa Jack and Judy, thank you for sending me a copy of your book, *Glorious Eternal Life in Heaven*. This book is very important and interesting. It is a blessing to me and to our church. I am writing to express my profound gratitude to my heavenly Father for all He has done in my life through this book. This book has helped me and several members of my church who long for a Holy Spirit revival in this town. Anyone facing a life or death struggle will be comforted by this book." (Kenya)

- This pastor said, "Warm greetings in the great name of our Lord and Savior Jesus Christ. Thank you very much for sending me your book, *Glorious Eternal Life in Heaven*. Would you please send me another copy of this book to give to a friend who is a pastor? Your books are my best resources to prepare my preaching and teaching into our local languages. By translating from your books into these languages, I can say that you are serving in many area churches. God bless you all." (Ethiopia)

Effective Prayer

- "I thank God for your book titled *Effective Prayer*. This book came to me at the right time. Since reading this book, God has done great wonders in my life and ministry. Our whole church is being affected by what we have learned about the power of prayer. I have read many books on prayer, but this one is unique. I no longer pray amiss. My prayer life has become much more effective. Your book has helped me to persevere in prayer much longer than before. This is a great book. I love it. I treasure this book. I do not know how to thank you. I pray that God will bless you both with long life and that you will enjoy the fruit of your labour." (Zambia)

- "Your book *Effective Prayer* is a great blessing to me. After reading this book I have so much more understanding about prayer. It is very easy to learn from all that you are teaching and all of the Scriptures in it. I now understand much more about the significance of prayer in my daily life, why I should pray and how to pray. You have enlightened my mind. I know that my loving Father wants me to pray all the time. I have learned to pray God's answer instead of focusing on the problem. This book is very vital to my daily life. I am so thankful to both of you for another great book for people who need answers. Thank you so much for the great understanding that I found in this book." (the Philippines)

- "I have been studying your book *Effective Prayer*. This book has inspired me to do a lot more praying. Praying to God is such a privilege. To know that God is just waiting for me to come and talk with Him is tremendous. The way you brought out the gift of being baptized in the Holy Spirit and praying in tongues will make it easier for people to receive this much-needed gift in their lives. Our pastor is using your book to teach on prayer. I have given copies of this book to many people in our church. I gave one to another pastor in our town. I love you both in the Lord Jesus Christ. I thank God for you and for allowing Him to continue to use you in the body of Christ." (Oklahoma)

Never, Never Give Up

- "I am a 68-year-old businessman. At my age I should be enjoying a life way past retirement. It is not so. In 1997 Thailand suffered a severe economic crunch and my business almost went down under. It took me many years to try to come back. Just as I thought I was climbing out of the black hole, another crisis hit two years ago. This time I am too old to fight, but I have no choice but to go on. I thought that God and I were very close. However, after the first crisis hit I sort of lost my faith along with my hope. After the second crisis hit, I thought that God had forsaken me. I all but lost my faith totally until one day a good friend gave me a book, *Never, Never Give Up*. At first I didn't want to read it. However, insisted by my friend, I did. I stayed up the whole night finishing the book. By morning I kneeled down and begged God to forgive me for my foolishness. I felt so ashamed for my behavior. I begged Him to accept me back. After I did that, I know that God has forgiven me. Now I am back to feeling close to Him again. I am so happy and grateful for this book. God is great!" (Thailand)

- "Thanks for being there when you are so much needed by all of us. After seven major operations I am beginning to walk again and help others which is the full purpose of my existence which Jesus Christ has set before me. Your book, *Never, Never Give Up*, stayed by my pillow along with my Bible while I was recuperating from these operations. When I re-read it, I was charged with peace and energy again. The pain diminishes and I can speak of God's infinite love and mercy to others who are facing similar trials. Thank you for writing this God-inspired book." (Florida)

- "Suicide has shown its face in my mind. I found myself falling deeper and deeper into the pit of hell. My life seemed so grim. I could not see where I could make a difference and was planning to believe that if I chose to leave this life it would not matter. When I received *Never, Never Give Up* I read the first three chapters that evening. When I arrived at page ninety, your verse changed my life. I want you to know that I have been delivered from this season of trial. I rededicated my life to the Lord and feel wonderful.

Thank you so much for your work. Through our Lord you have saved my life. Thank you for my life back." (Texas)

Reverent Awe of God
- "Greetings in the mighty name of our Lord Jesus. Thank you for sending me a free copy of *Reverent Awe of God*. I was surprised to learn your ages when I read this book. You are still relevant in your books. You are changing the destiny of many people globally. I will use this book to teach our church members from the many valuable lessons that I have learned from your book. May God bless you and supply all of your needs." (Kenya)
- "A student in one of the universities read your book, *Reverent Awe of God,* from our library. As a result, she was converted from the Muslim religion to Christianity. She said that the concept of our Christian faith is more real. She can see that God is her Father and that Jesus Christ is real and the only Son of God. This student said that she is facing attacks and rejections from her home. She needs our prayers. Papa, thank you." (Ghana)
- "We are very grateful for the box of books you sent us. I praise God for your new book, *Reverent Awe of God*. This book can really help any believer to establish a genuine relationship with our Maker. When we read your books and consider your age, we thank God that the Spirit of God never grows old. May God continue to bless you and give you long life so that you will write many more books that explain the Word of God to us." (Ghana)

Overcoming Fear

- "Thank you for sending your books to the Philippines. I was very blessed to read *Overcoming Fear*. This book explained the sources of fear and what I should do to overcome fear. It is really a blessing to know all of this information that helped me to overcome the fear I have felt all these years. I have cherished every chapter in the book. It has become food for my soul. Thank you so much for explaining all of this so well. I have learned that I should never be afraid of anyone because I can be absolutely certain that God lives in my heart. This is great assurance because I know that God is greater than anything I will ever face in this life. This book has been a great blessing in my life. God bless you both." (the Philippines)

- "I want to thank you immediately for your new book, *Overcoming Fear*. I have read every one of your books and given copies to many people, but I want to tell you that I believe this is your best book ever. I can hardly put it down. The day I received it I stayed up late, even though I was very tired, to read the first four chapters. The next morning I read two more chapters before going to work. This book is very inspiring. It gives me great peace. God's peace is so great that I cannot describe it. I have almost finished reading this book. When I am done, I will immediately read it again. Enclosed is a check for ten copies of this book plus a contribution to Lamplight Ministries. Thank you, Jack and Judy, for writing this wonderful book." (Massachusetts)

- "I want to thank you for publishing the book *Overcoming Fear*. I am reading mine for the second time. I cannot tell you how comforting it is. The way you have put information along with the right Bible verses is so truly helpful. As world conditions worsen, I can tell you that this book will be a constant companion alongside my Bible. I am so grateful for you both. Keep up the good work. You are making a big difference in peoples' lives. You have in mine." (Minnesota)

Victory Over Adversity
- "I am a pure and proud Dutchman married to a Tanzanian woman. I have had a lot of problems staying with an African wife in Europe. I love my wife so much, but the environment for my wife was not good enough in terms of getting a job. This affected us very much to the extent that I was even planning to relocate to Tanzania for the sake of my wife and children's future. Thank God that an angel was sent to me by the name of Jim who gave me a book, *Victory over Adversity*. This book is amazing and great. It contains the answers to my problems and is a great encouragement to me. As a Dutchman I find it very interesting to read a book with simple English. Putting the facts of this book into practice has changed my life greatly. I have found a new job. My wife has found a good job. The thoughts of relocating to Tanzania have faded. My faith has increased and my commitment to God has grown. I pray that God will bless the writers of this book and also the man who gave me this book. My wife and I are always reading this book. It is our source of strength." (Holland)

- "I praise God for His living Word. Thank you for the books that you have sent to China. You cannot imagine what *Victory over Adversity* did in my life as a young believer. Not only is the language clear and accessible, but the content is very rewarding. I learned a lot from this book. I now meditate day and night on the Word of God. I am in the presence of God often. I am confident that I can overcome any adversity in the precious name of Jesus Christ. May God bless you and fill you with His infinite grace, Mr. Jack and his wife." (China)

- "I am a 22-year-old college student in Thailand. My family is half Christian. My mother is a Christian whereas my father is a Buddhist. I am the eldest daughter of my parents with one younger brother and sister. All three of us have been baptized as Christians since birth. Frankly, I have never had much faith in God and always have had problems with both of my parents. I think that they don't understand me. They think I don't listen to them. Last month my mother was given a book, *Victory over Adversity,* by her friend. Out of curiosity I took the book and read it before she did. I could not put it down. For the first time I felt that God is real and is close to me. I cried and cried and felt sorry for my past behavior toward God and my parents. I went to my mother and apologized, to her great surprise. Now I go to church with her every Sunday. I am very thankful to my mother's friend who gave her this book and also to the writers of this book who have changed my life and brought me to God which my mother could not do. Thank you both!" (Thailand)

- "*Exchange Your Worries for God's Perfect Peace* is a masterpiece. I am reading this book to the people here in the Philippines. I saw tears flowing down their faces as I read them parts of this book. I must get this book translated into their language. I am reading this book for the second time. After 30 years in the ministry I have finally learned how to turn my worries over to God. I have learned more from this book in the last few months than I have ever learned in my life. I will not allow my copy of this book to leave my presence. I thank God for you." (the Philippines)

- "I just want to tell you how much I appreciate you and your excellent book, *Exchange Your Worries for God's Perfect Peace*. I have read all of your books several times each. I continually go back to refer to the notes I have made in your books. I have done this for close to 15 years and pages are falling out of your books. I read the Bible daily. Your books are a close second to the Bible. I have never found another Christian author who teaches me more about God's Word and speaks directly to my heart as your writings do. Thank you for helping me appreciate and respect the Word of God." (Wisconsin)

- "I was in despair struggling with my life and ministry. *Exchange Your Worries for God's Perfect Peace* has strengthened me and encouraged my heart. My country is often threatened by disasters. Your book and the Scripture in it has helped me to focus on God, no matter what circumstances I have experienced and will face in the future. The language in the book is very clear and easy to understand for someone like me who uses English as a second language. I have been blessed by reading this book. My faith in Jesus has increased. Thank you for sending this book to me. I thank God that I know you. You are a blessing." (Indonesia)

God's Joy Regardless of Circumstances
- "*God's Joy Regardless of Circumstances* came to me right on time. Being in prison for 20 years for a crime I didn't commit and then having to deal with severe family problems is not a morsel that is easy to swallow. My oldest daughter was pregnant and we were looking forward to having my first grandson born. We were very pained to learn that my daughter had to lose her baby. In the midst of dealing with this problem, you sent me a free copy of *God's Joy Regardless of Circumstances*. When I avidly started to read this book, my daughter underwent surgery, lost her baby and faced uncertainty and despair. *God's Joy Regardless of Circumstances* pulled us through. Thank you also for sending a free copy of this book to my daughter. May God continue blessing Lamplight Ministries." (Florida)
- "Many thanks for sending me *God's Joy Regardless of Circumstances*. This book has been a real stream in the desert that I have been able to drink from. I have been blessed tremendously by this book. My life has not been the same since I started reading it. I have used this book to help many people on my radio programme every Sunday. Many people have given their lives to Christ because of these messages." (Zambia)

- "Only this year I faced a lot of challenges. As a result I became bitter at heart. The wonderful Scripture verses in *God's Joy Regardless of Circumstances* took away my bitterness. I am happy now. This book has instructed me how to handle any situation with God's joy. I now can see God's solution to my life challenges by the presence of God's joy inside me. Your God-given insight has given new meaning to my spiritual life. Thank you for the encouragement through your writings." (Lome-Togo West Africa)

God's Wisdom Is Available to You
- "I did not sleep last night after reading your book *God's Wisdom is Available to You.* Thank you for your wonderful work. Because of persecution against my ministry, I spent a considerable amount of time in the hospital because of depression. I am now well and healthy in Jesus' name. Thank you for your help. I will be teaching members of my church from key text in your book. Please be my mentor, teacher and counselor." (Ghana)
- "I thank God each and every day for Jack and Judy Hartman. When I started reading your book on wisdom, everything was going wrong in my life. This book revived my spirit and my faith in God. It has changed my life. The Bible used to be like Greek to me. Now I can read it and understand it. I can't put this book down because I know I need to absorb it. I'm going through it for a second time. This book is one of the best things that has ever happened to me. I thank you both and I thank God." (Florida)
- "You did a fantastic job on this book. It is an encyclopedia on God's wisdom. The writing style is

just great. Many books don't bring the reader through the subject the way this book does. I'm very impressed with that. You have made it a real joy for me to study and re-digest Scripture. This book has been very good for me." (North Carolina)

A Close and Intimate Relationship with God

- "Your book, *A Close and Intimate Relationship with God,* is tremendous. I thought that I had a close relationship with God, but this book really opened my eyes. I now can see many things that I still need to do to be even closer to God. I couldn't put this book down. When I had to stop reading, I couldn't wait to get back to it the next day. Every chapter is filled with Scripture that is very helpful to me. I will be making many changes in my life as a result of reading this awesome book. Thank you and God bless you." (New Hampshire)

- "Thank you for giving me a copy of your book *A Close and Intimate Relationship with God.* This book is written so clearly that all instructions are to the point. My life has been greatly changed and refreshed. The presence of God has become very strong in my life. I am at peace trusting my God to meet every need. My mind is totally on God. I can clearly hear His voice. I am receiving guidance and direction from Him as a result of this book. I cannot afford to spend a day without reading this book. I carry it with me wherever I go." (Zambia)

- "Thank you for your book titled *A Close and Intimate Relationship with God.* This inspiring book helped me to draw closer to our heavenly Father. In Chapter 25 you said that Paul and Silas were praising God in prison. I was having a challenging day when I read this chapter. God spoke through your book to praise Him no matter what circumstances I faced. Thank you for that inspiration. The information on dying to self in the last chapter where Paul said that he dies daily really encouraged me. I am learning to do much better putting God first, others second and myself last. Thank you at Lamplight Ministries for the thousands of people around the world that you are supporting. May the dear Lord bless you abundantly." (China)

Unshakable Faith in Almighty God
• "I thank God for the book *Unshakable Faith in Almighty God*. Because I am not indigenous Chinese, it is not easy to fellowship with the local Chinese. When I got this book I was able to see a way in the wilderness. It became my guide and light every day. When I was just about to give up Christianity, God at the right time provided this book to me. The truths and clear instruction in this book are direct from the throne of God. I am determined to move on with God come what may. I praise God that is He able to raise people we have never seen like Jack and Judy Hartman to speak into our lives through their publications. God bless the Hartman family. One day when Christ comes it will be exciting for them to see how they have influenced the world for God in Jesus' name. I am so grateful for these free books that cost a lot of money in publishing, printing and postage." (China)
• "I have been pastoring in Belgium for the past 15 years. In the past our church was flourishing and

doing very well until late last year when my praise and worship leader decided to break away and form another church. This was a very big blow to us as a church. Most of our strong and committed members left the church with some of the church instruments. My wife almost gave up. She was discouraged. This also affected our finances. Pastor Jim gave me a book titled *Unshakable Faith in Almighty God*. Before I read this book my faith was shaken and I almost gave up. This book took me step by step to show me how to make my faith grow. You cannot read this book and remain the same. I have been using the book to preach to the few members that remain with us. In the past four months we have experienced revival. The anointing is so strong and the members have been strengthened so much through the preaching from this book. We are determined to not give up. God bless the Hartmans for being a blessing to us in Europe." (Belgium)

- "*Unshakable Faith in Almighty God* has amazed me. The language is so simple and very clear to understand. This book is powerful and life-changing. I will always hang on to this book. Brother Hartman, God's favour and wisdom are so great on your life. I believe this book is written on very heavy anointing from God. Your reward in heaven will be so great. All those who have sown seeds in your ministry should rejoice. When I wake up, I read this book. Before going to bed, I read it. I will continue to go through it again and again. Your ministry is a big blessing to me. You are always in our prayers." (Zambia)

How to Study the Bible

- "Your book, *How to Study the Bible*, is a gem. Since I became a Christian 41 years ago, I have studied the Bible using a variety of methods. Your method is simple and straightforward. It involves hard work, but the rewards are real. I have read several of your books and this book is the one I would highly recommend to any Christian because this book is the foundation. God bless you, brother." (England)

- "My wife and I are utilizing the Bible study method that you explained in *How to Study the Bible*. We are really growing spiritually as a result. Our old methods of study were not nearly as fruitful. Thank you for writing about your method." (Idaho)

- "I have read almost all of your books and they are outstanding. The one that blessed me the most was *How to Study the Bible*. The study part was excellent, but the meditation chapters were very, very beneficial. I am indebted to you for sharing these. I purchased 30 copies to give to friends. Every earnest student of God's Word needs a copy." (Tennessee)

Increased Energy and Vitality

- "It is so great to meet Christians on the same wave length. In your book *Increased Energy and Vitality*, you are writing almost word for word in some cases what I have been saying to patients for almost 30 years." (Ohio)

- "Last year I obtained a copy of your book *Increased Energy and Vitality*. My wife and I have read and have in fact changed our ways of eating and drinking and exercising because of your influence. We thoroughly appreciate this God-centered message that is so well presented. I have enclosed an order for more of these books. We know many people we wish to help. This is the first step in spreading the news you have so generously put together. Thank you for your efforts. May God continue your leadership in writing, speaking and guidance." (Illinois)

- "I have benefited tremendously from reading and personally applying the principles learned from your book *Increased Energy and Vitality.* By applying your methods, I have gained additional energy especially during my low periods from 2:00 p.m. to 4:00 p.m. I highly recommend your book to others. Keep up the good work." (Florida)

100 Years from Today

- "*100 Years From Today* told me that going to church and doing good deeds won't get me to heaven. I believe in Jesus Christ. I believe He died for our sins and that He forgives us for what we did wrong. Heaven is where I belong. I am born again. I have a new life. This book has changed my life." (Florida)

- "I am writing to express my deep and profound appreciation for your book *100 Years from Today.* I recently began attending a Bible-based church where I found a copy of this book in their lending library. I read the book in one sitting, reading the words aloud to myself. Your book explained details from the Bible that I had not learned before. I thank you for taking the time and effort to write this book. My written words can never fully express how grateful I am to you. By my actions, a changed life and a deep sense of peace, I hope to bear fruit by helping others." (Massachusetts)

- "I find it hard to put *100 Years from Today* down. I read the whole book in a day and a half. I never knew how much pain and suffering Jesus went through to pay for my sins. I learned how much He loves us." (Florida)

Nuggets of Faith

- "Your books, tapes and meditation cards are really a blessing to me. They came at just the right time. I am preparing sermons on faith from *Nuggets of Faith*. I want the congregation to be constantly learning God's Word in order to have much more faith. I also have been encouraged personally through that book. It is awesome. Thank you for your powerful and inspiring publications." (Zambia)

- "We give *Nuggets of Faith* to people who are hospitalized, for birthdays, to saved and unsaved. Everyone who has received one tells us 'It's the best little book I've ever read. It's so clear and easy to understand.'" (Indiana)

- "I work as a store manager. Today I was told that I was no longer needed. Praise Jesus that only two months prior to this date I had accepted the Lord Jesus as my personal Lord and Savior. I have faith that the Lord was working to bring me to a new direction. I am writing to thank you for your excellent book *Nuggets of Faith*. The moment I arrived home after having been dismissed, I received this book in the mail. I completed this short but awesome book in a little over two hours. It has helped my faith to grow stronger and I know that I will begin a great new journey tomorrow. God bless you." (New York)

Comments on our Scripture Meditation Cards

- "My back was hurting so badly that I couldn't get comfortable. I was miserable whether I sat or stood or laid down. I didn't know what to do. Suddenly I thought of the Scripture cards on healing that my husband had purchased. I decided to meditate on the Scripture in these cards. I was only on the second card when, all of a sudden, I felt heat go from my neck down through my body. The Lord had healed me. I never knew it could happen so fast. The pain has not come back." (Idaho)

- "My wife and I use your Scripture cards every day when we pray. I read the card for that day in English and then my wife repeats it in Norwegian. We then pray based upon the Scripture reference on that day's card. These cards have been very beneficial to us. We would like to see the Scripture cards published in the Norwegian language." (Norway)

- "Your Scripture cards have been very helpful to my wife and myself. We have taped them to the walls in our home and we meditate on them constantly. I also take four or five cards with me every day when I go to work. I meditate on them while I drive. The Scripture on these cards is a constant source of encouragement to us. We ask for permission to translate *Trust God for Your Finances*. This book is badly needed by the people in Turkey." (This permission was granted.) (Turkey)

- "My mom is 95 years old. She was in the Bergen-Belsen Concentration Camp in Germany from 1943 to 1945. She has always had a lot of worry and fear. My mother was helped greatly in overcoming this problem by your Scripture cards titled *Freedom from Worry and Fear*. She was helped so much that she asked me to order another set to give to a friend." (California)

- "I am overwhelmed about the revelations in your Scripture Meditation Cards. These Scripture cards have helped me so much that I cannot write enough on this sheet of paper. We have gone through a five-day programme in our church using the Scripture cards. My faith has increased tremendously. I no longer am submitting to my own will and desires, but I am now submitting to the will of God and it is so fantastic. God bless you, Jack and Judy Hartman." (Ghana)

- "I am very enthusiastic about your Scripture cards and your tape titled *Receive Healing from the Lord*. I love your tape. The clarity of your voice and your sincerity and compassion will encourage sick people. They can listen to this tape throughout the day, before they go to sleep at night, while they are driving to the doctor's office, in the hospital, etc. The tape is filled with Scripture and many good comments on Scripture. This cassette tape and your Scripture cards on healing are powerful tools that will help many sick people." (Tennessee) (NOTE:

The ten cassette tapes for our Scripture Meditation Cards are available on 60-minute CDs as well.)

- "I meditate constantly on the healing cards and listen to your tape on healing over and over. Your voice is so soothing. You are a wonderful teacher. My faith is increasing constantly." (New Hampshire).

- "I thank God for you. I carry your Scripture Meditation Cards in my purse. The Scriptures you have chosen are all powerful. What a blessing to be able to meditate on the Word of God at any time, anywhere. Thank you for your hard work. The Scripture cards are a blessing to me." (Canada)

ORDER FORM FOR BOOKS

Book Title	Quantity	Total
What Does God Say? ($18)	_____x $18 =	_____
God Lives in the Heart of Every Christian ($14)	_____x $14 =	_____
The Rapture and the Second Coming of Christ ($14)	_____x $14 =	_____
Live Continually in the Presence of God ($14)	_____x $14 =	_____
Glorious Eternal Life in Heaven ($14)	_____x $14 =	_____
Reverent Awe of God ($14)	_____x $14 =	_____
God's Plan for Your Life ($14)	_____x $14 =	_____
You Can Hear the Voice of God ($14)	_____x $14 =	_____
God's Instructions for Growing Older ($14)	_____x $14 =	_____
Effective Prayer ($14)	_____x $14 =	_____
Overcoming Fear ($14)	_____x $14 =	_____
A Close and Intimate Relationship with God ($14)	_____x $14 =	_____
God's Joy Regardless of Circumstances ($14)	_____x $14 =	_____
Victory Over Adversity ($14)	_____x $14 =	_____
Receive Healing from the Lord ($14)	_____x $14 =	_____
Unshakable Faith in Almighty God ($14)	_____x $14 =	_____
Exchange Your Worries for God's Perfect Peace ($14)	_____x $14 =	_____
God's Wisdom is Available to You ($14)	_____x $14 =	_____
Quiet Confidence in the Lord ($14)	_____x $14 =	_____
Never, Never Give Up ($14)	_____x $14 =	_____
Increased Energy and Vitality ($14)	_____x $14 =	_____
Trust God For Your Finances ($14)	_____x $14 =	_____
How to Study the Bible ($10)	_____x $10 =	_____
Nuggets of Faith ($10)	_____x $10 =	_____
100 Years From Today ($10)	_____x $10 =	_____

Price of books _____

Minus 40% discount for 5-9 books _____

Minus 50% discount for 10 or more books _____

Net price of order _____

Add 15% **before discount** for shipping and handling _____

Florida residents only, add 7% sales tax _____

Tax deductible contribution to Lamplight Ministries, Inc. _____

Enclosed check or money order (do not send cash) _____

(Foreign orders must be submitted in U.S. dollars.)

Please make check payable to **Lamplight Ministries, Inc**. and mail to:
PO Box 1307, Dunedin, FL 34697

MC_____ Visa_____ AmEx_____ Disc._____ Card # _____

Exp Date _____ 3-digit code _____ Signature _____

Name _____

Address _____

City _____ Phone _____

State or Province _____ Zip or Postal Code _____

Email _____ Website: _____

ORDER FORM FOR BOOKS

Book Title	Quantity	Total
What Does God Say? ($18)	_____x $18 =	_____
God Lives in the Heart of Every Christian ($14)	_____x $14 =	_____
The Rapture and the Second Coming of Christ ($14)	_____x $14 =	_____
Live Continually in the Presence of God ($14)	_____x $14 =	_____
Glorious Eternal Life in Heaven ($14)	_____x $14 =	_____
Reverent Awe of God ($14)	_____x $14 =	_____
God's Plan for Your Life ($14)	_____x $14 =	_____
You Can Hear the Voice of God ($14)	_____x $14 =	_____
God's Instructions for Growing Older ($14)	_____x $14 =	_____
Effective Prayer ($14)	_____x $14 =	_____
Overcoming Fear ($14)	_____x $14 =	_____
A Close and Intimate Relationship with God ($14)	_____x $14 =	_____
God's Joy Regardless of Circumstances ($14)	_____x $14 =	_____
Victory Over Adversity ($14)	_____x $14 =	_____
Receive Healing from the Lord ($14)	_____x $14 =	_____
Unshakable Faith in Almighty God ($14)	_____x $14 =	_____
Exchange Your Worries for God's Perfect Peace ($14)	_____x $14 =	_____
God's Wisdom is Available to You ($14)	_____x $14 =	_____
Quiet Confidence in the Lord ($14)	_____x $14 =	_____
Never, Never Give Up ($14)	_____x $14 =	_____
Increased Energy and Vitality ($14)	_____x $14 =	_____
Trust God For Your Finances ($14)	_____x $14 =	_____
How to Study the Bible ($10)	_____x $10 =	_____
Nuggets of Faith ($10)	_____x $10 =	_____
100 Years From Today ($10)	_____x $10 =	_____

Price of books _____

Minus 40% discount for 5-9 books _____

Minus 50% discount for 10 or more books _____

Net price of order _____

Add 15% **before discount** for shipping and handling _____

Florida residents only, add 7% sales tax _____

Tax deductible contribution to Lamplight Ministries, Inc. _____

Enclosed check or money order (do not send cash) _____

(Foreign orders must be submitted in U.S. dollars.)

Please make check payable to **Lamplight Ministries, Inc.** and mail to:
PO Box 1307, Dunedin, FL 34697

MC_____ Visa_____ AmEx_____ Disc._____ Card # _____

Exp Date _____ 3-digit code _____ Signature _____

Name _____

Address _____

City _____ Phone _____

State or Province _____ Zip or Postal Code _____

Email _____ Website: _____

ORDER FORM FOR SCRIPTURE MEDITATION CARDS AND CDs

SCRIPTURE MEDITATION CARDS	QUANTITY	PRICE
A Closer Relationship with the Lord ($5)	_____	_____
Continually Increasing Faith in God ($5)	_____	_____
Enjoy God's Wonderful Peace ($5)	_____	_____
Financial Instructions from God ($5)	_____	_____
Find God's Will for Your Life ($5)	_____	_____
Freedom from Worry and Fear ($5)	_____	_____
God is Always with You ($5)	_____	_____
Our Father's Wonderful Love ($5)	_____	_____
Receive God's Blessing in Adversity ($5)	_____	_____
Receive Healing from the Lord ($5)	_____	_____

CDs	QUANTITY	PRICE
A Closer Relationship with the Lord ($10)	_____	_____
Continually Increasing Faith in God ($10)	_____	_____
Enjoy God's Wonderful Peace ($10)	_____	_____
Financial Instructions from God ($10)	_____	_____
Find God's Will for Your Life ($10)	_____	_____
Freedom from Worry and Fear ($10)	_____	_____
God is Always with You ($10)	_____	_____
Our Father's Wonderful Love ($10)	_____	_____
Receive God's Blessing in Adversity ($10)	_____	_____
Receive Healing from the Lord ($10)	_____	_____

TOTAL PRICE _____

Minus 40% discount for 5-9 Scripture Cards and CDs _____
Minus 50% discount for 10 or more Scripture Cards and CDs _____
Net price of order _____
Add 15% **before discount** for shipping and handling _____
Florida residents only, add 7% sales tax _____
Tax deductible contribution to Lamplight Ministries, Inc. _____
Enclosed check or money order (do not send cash) _____
(Foreign orders must be submitted in U.S. dollars.)

Please make check payable to **Lamplight Ministries, Inc.** and mail to:
PO Box 1307, Dunedin, FL 34697

MC_____ Visa_____ AmEx_____ Disc._____ Card # _____

Exp Date _____ 3-digit code _____ Signature _____

Name _____

Address _____

City _____ Phone _____

State or Province _____ Zip or Postal Code _____

Email _____ Website: _____

ORDER FORM FOR SCRIPTURE MEDITATION CARDS AND CDs

SCRIPTURE MEDITATION CARDS	QUANTITY	PRICE
A Closer Relationship with the Lord ($5)	_____	_____
Continually Increasing Faith in God ($5)	_____	_____
Enjoy God's Wonderful Peace ($5)	_____	_____
Financial Instructions from God ($5)	_____	_____
Find God's Will for Your Life ($5)	_____	_____
Freedom from Worry and Fear ($5)	_____	_____
God is Always with You ($5)	_____	_____
Our Father's Wonderful Love ($5)	_____	_____
Receive God's Blessing in Adversity ($5)	_____	_____
Receive Healing from the Lord ($5)	_____	_____

CDs	QUANTITY	PRICE
A Closer Relationship with the Lord ($10)	_____	_____
Continually Increasing Faith in God ($10)	_____	_____
Enjoy God's Wonderful Peace ($10)	_____	_____
Financial Instructions from God ($10)	_____	_____
Find God's Will for Your Life ($10)	_____	_____
Freedom from Worry and Fear ($10)	_____	_____
God is Always with You ($10)	_____	_____
Our Father's Wonderful Love ($10)	_____	_____
Receive God's Blessing in Adversity ($10)	_____	_____
Receive Healing from the Lord ($10)	_____	_____

TOTAL PRICE _____

Minus 40% discount for 5-9 Scripture Cards and CDs _____

Minus 50% discount for 10 or more Scripture Cards and CDs _____

Net price of order _____

Add 15% **before discount** for shipping and handling _____

Florida residents only, add 7% sales tax _____

Tax deductible contribution to Lamplight Ministries, Inc. _____

Enclosed check or money order (do not send cash) _____

(Foreign orders must be submitted in U.S. dollars.)

Please make check payable to **Lamplight Ministries, Inc**. and mail to:
PO Box 1307, Dunedin, FL 34697

MC_____ Visa_____ AmEx_____ Disc._____ Card # _____

Exp Date _____ 3-digit code _____ Signature _____

Name _____

Address _____

City _____ Phone _____

State or Province _____ Zip or Postal Code _____

Email _____ Website: _____

www.ingramcontent.com/pod-product-compliance
Lightning Source LLC
LaVergne TN
LVHW051124080426
835510LV00018B/2221